United States v. Amistad:

SLAVE SHIP MUTINY

United States v. Amistad:

Slave Ship Mutiny

SUSAN DUDLEY GOLD

Marshall Cavendish
Benchmark
New York

To Mark Dudley and Marlene Aulten, who truly
cherish freedom

*With thanks to researcher Lee Burnett for his dedication and
excellence in assisting with this book. With special thanks to
Professor David M. O'Brien of the Woodrow Wilson
Department of Politics at the University of Virginia for
reviewing the text of this book.*

Marshall Cavendish Benchmark
99 White Plains Road
Tarrytown, NY 10591
www.marshallcavendish.us

Library of Congress Cataloging-in-Publication Data
Gold, Susan Dudley.
United States v. Amistad : slave ship mutiny / by Susan Dudley Gold.
p. cm. -- (Supreme Court milestones)
Includes bibliographical references and index.
ISBN-13: 978-0-7614-2143-6
ISBN-10: 0-7614-2143-2
1. Cinque--Trials, litigation, etc.--Juvenile literature. 2. Trials (Mutiny)--United
States--Juvenile literature. 3. Fugitive slaves--Legal status, laws, etc.--United States-
-Juvenile literature. 4. Slave insurrections--United States--Juvenile literature. 5.
Amistad (Schooner)--Juvenile literature. I. Title. II. Series.
KF223.C56G65 2006
343.73'0874--dc22
2006003086

Photo research by Candlepants Incorporated

Cover Photo: The New Haven Colony Historical Society

The photographs in this book are used by permission and through the courtesy of:
The New Haven Colony Historical Society: 1, 2, 3, 13, 14, 68,104. *Corbis*: Fine Art
Photographic Library, 6; 27, 40, 45, 48, 110; Bettmann, 29, 65, 79, 82. *The Connecticut
Historical Society, Hartford, Connecticut*: 17, 113. *New York Public Library*: Humanities
and Social Sciences Library/Print Collection, Mirium and Ira D. Wallach Division of
Art, Prints and Photographs, 21, 93. *Bridgeman Art Library*: Musee desArts d'Afrique et
d'Oceanie, Paris /Giraudon, 34. *Beinecke Rare Book and Manuscript Library, Yale
University*: 55. *Art Resource, NY*: National Portrait Gallery, Smithsonian Institution: 75.

Editorial Director: Michelle Bisson
Art Director: Anahid Hamparian
Series Designer: Sonia Chaghatzbanian

Printed in China
1 3 5 6 4 2

contents

A SHIP APPROACHES MORO CASTLE AT THE ENTRANCE TO HAVANA BAY IN HAVANA, CUBA. THE CITY SERVED AS A MAJOR MARKETPLACE FOR THE SLAVE TRADE IN THE AMERICAS DURING THE LATE 1700S AND 1800S.

Introduction
"Make Us Free"

In 1841, two decades before America's Civil War, the U.S. Supreme Court ruled that blacks illegally enslaved by white traders had the right to be free. The decision itself was a narrow one, targeting the slave trade rather than slavery. Nevertheless, the case, *United States* v. *Amistad*, focused attention on the issue of slavery just as politicians were trying to avoid discussing the divisive topic. Although the United States had banned the importation of slaves in 1808 and many other nations had followed suit by 1820, the lucrative trade continued unabated. Slavery itself was embedded in the nation's economy and had been part of American life for more than two centuries. Southern planters depended on slaves to harvest cotton, the nation's largest export. Even though many Americans considered slavery morally wrong, they feared that banning it would disrupt U.S. prosperity and trigger violent opposition in the South. Politicians did not want to alienate Southern voters by taking a stand against slavery. Abolitionists who dared to speak out on the subject were attacked, ridiculed, and shunned.

The *Amistad* case—one of the first "civil rights" suits to be heard by the U.S. Supreme Court—revolved around a group of Africans captured by slave traders and transported to Cuba and then the United States. After the ship sailed from Havana, the Africans revolted, killed the captain and the cook, and took control of the ship *Amistad*. Led by a young man known as Cinque, the Africans commandeered the ship and ordered two Spanish slave traders aboard to take them back to Africa. Instead, the *Amistad*—meaning "friendship" in Spanish—sailed into U.S. waters and anchored off Long Island, where American naval officers took over the ship and its passengers.

The ensuing legal battles over the ship, its cargo, and the Africans on board became front-page news in two nations. The case pitted a former U.S. president against the current president, threatened relations between Spain and the United States, and escalated tensions between proslavery Southerners and antislavery Northerners. Spain claimed ownership of the ship and the enslaved Africans on behalf of its citizens. The U.S. government, under the direction of President Martin Van Buren, filed the claim in court on Spain's behalf and later appealed the lower court's decision. The Africans, represented by antislavery lawyers, claimed their right to freedom. Abolitionists financed the legal battle and used the case to take a stand against slavery. Former president John Quincy Adams carried the Africans' appeal to the high court.

The U.S. Supreme Court eventually settled the case. In an 8 to 1 decision, the Court ruled that the Africans should be freed. "The United States are bound to respect their [the Africans'] rights as much as those of Spanish subjects," the Court ruled.

The decision turned out to be more of a blow to the slave trade than to slavery itself. Nevertheless, abolitionists celebrated the ruling as the first to acknowledge that blacks had rights that must be respected. It would be decades, however, before the U.S. government would begin enforcing those rights for black Americans.

Internationally, the effect of the *Amistad* decision extended across the ocean to Africa and Spain. The ruling gave new momentum to American missionary efforts in Africa. It also helped spur interest in the African independence movement, which eventually resulted in a colony of free American blacks in Africa. Angered by the Court's decision, Spain harbored resentment against America and continued to demand compensation for the loss of the ship and the slaves for the next twenty years.

For many Americans, the *Amistad* case presented ethical, moral, and legal questions left unanswered by the narrow Court decision. To the imprisoned Africans, however, the ruling was a life-or-death matter, which eventually freed them to return home. Kale, the young African boy who was among the *Amistad* prisoners and learned English during captivity, wrote of his people's anguish and their yearning to be free in a letter to John Quincy Adams while the Africans waited for the Court to hear their case:

> Dear friend Mr. Adams, you have children, you have friends, you love them, you feel sorry if Mendi people come and take all to Africa. We feel bad for our friends, and our friends all feel bad for us. . . . We want you to tell court that Mendi people no want to go back to Havana, we no want to be killed. Dear Friend, we want you to know how we feel. . . . All we want is make us free.

In 1842, after money had been raised for their passage, thirty-five of the freed *Amistad* captives returned to their homeland in Africa.

John P. Norton, one of the founders of the Connecticut Anti-Slavery Society, called the decision "a great triumph of law and justice." As abolitionists had hoped, the decision bolstered the antislavery cause. It united the various factions of the movement and won support from Americans influenced by the sympathetic newspaper reports of the captives. It also added to the nation's growing rupture over the issue of slavery that ultimately led to the Civil War.

During his arguments in the case, Roger Baldwin, the Africans' lawyer, asserted that the Declaration of Independence guaranteed all people the natural right to be free. That proposition would serve as the foundation of Abraham Lincoln's Gettysburg Address, given more than twenty years later in the midst of the Civil War. And finally, slavery would fall.

In late August 1839, a long black schooner with tattered sails appeared off the coast of Long Island. The ship, the *Amistad*, raised suspicions immediately. No flag flew from the mast, and barnacles and sea grass covered the vessel's hull. Aboard, a group of black men and children gathered on the deck, some naked and others wearing silk shirts and pantaloons. A few of the leaders, armed with pistols and swords, directed other vessels away.

On August 26, several of the men left the vessel to get supplies ashore. Clad in blankets and wearing necklaces made of gold doubloons, the men came upon two sea captains, Peletiah Fordham and Henry Green. The captains promised to help the group sail to Africa in exchange for the gold stored on the vessel. Before Fordham and Green could board the ship, however, a nearby U.S. Coast Guard brig, the USS *Washington*, took control of the vessel. The crew of the *Washington*, under the command of Lieutenant Thomas Gedney and armed with pistols, herded everyone below deck. The men on shore were also taken into custody.

Two Spaniards on board greeted the officers with great relief. The younger one, Jose Ruiz, who spoke English, told the chilling story of the blacks' mutiny at sea. His account, as related in the *New London Gazette*, horrified those who heard it. The schooner *Amistad* had left Havana two months before with fifty-four black slaves. Its destination was Port Principe, Cuba, about 240 nautical miles away. The trip usually took about three days, but bad weather delayed the journey. On the fourth day at sea, the blacks had seized control of the ship, killing the captain and the cook. Two other crew members apparently fled overboard. The mutineers spared the lives of Ruiz and his companion, Pedro Montes, so that the Spaniards could sail the ship to Africa for them.

Ruiz claimed the slaves came from Cuba, which was then under Spanish rule. He said he had bought forty-nine males, and Montes, the older Spaniard, had bought three girls and a boy. Another slave, Antonio, served the captain as cabin boy. Ten of the captives died during the voyage; two were killed in the revolt, and the others died from illness and disease.

Ruiz identified a young, muscular black man as leader of the revolt. Sengbe Pieh, or Cinque as he came to be known in the press, was described as "about five foot eight, 25 or 26 years of age, of erect figure, well built, and very active. He is said to be a match for any two men aboard the schooner." A newspaper reporter for the *New London* (Connecticut) *Gazette* estimated that slave buyers would pay "at least $1,500" for Cinque at auction in New Orleans.

Cinque had forced loose a nail that secured his chains, freed himself and the other captives, and armed them with small knives stored with the sugarcane being transported aboard the ship. Ruiz said he and Montes had been spared only because the blacks needed them to navigate and steer the ship.

"The situation of the two whites was all this time truly deplorable, being treated with the greatest severity, and Pedro Montes, who had charge of the navigation, was suffering from two severe wounds, one in the head

A PORTRAIT OF SENGBE PIEH, OR CINQUE, THE YOUNG AFRICAN MAN WHO BECAME THE LEADER OF THE *AMISTAD* CAPTIVES.

and one in the arm, their lives threatened every instant," the article from the *New London Gazette* stated.

By day, the Spaniards steered the ship east toward Africa, but at night when the blacks had no sun to guide them, Montes and Ruiz secretly steered the boat back toward land "always in hopes of falling in with some vessel of war, or being enabled to run into some port, when they

A FANCIFUL ILLUSTRATION OF THE MUTINY ABOARD THE *AMISTAD*. THE ENSLAVED AFRICANS KILLED THE CAPTAIN AND THE COOK AND TOOK OVER THE SHIP. TWO OTHER CREW MEMBERS REPORTEDLY ESCAPED OVER THE SIDE. THE MUTINEERS SPARED THE LIVES OF TWO SPANISH SLAVEHOLDERS ABOARD AND ORDERED THEM TO SAIL THE VESSEL TO AFRICA.

would be relieved from their horrid situation." The blacks discovered the ruse when Long Island came into view.

After Ruiz finished his account, Gedney ordered the *Amistad* and its occupants taken to New Haven harbor in Connecticut. Some observers theorized that Gedney chose that port because Connecticut allowed slavery and would consider the commander's claim to the slaves aboard the *Amistad*. New York had freed all slaves in that state (except for visitors' slaves) by 1827.

Based on Ruiz's account of events, officers in New Haven arrested the black men who had been aboard the *Amistad* and charged them with piracy and murder. The entire group, including the children, was then taken to the New Haven jail. Thus began a new battle—this one fought in the courts—waged over property rights and personal freedom.

Great Excitement

The captives and the story of the mutiny caused great excitement among the residents of New Haven and surrounding towns. There were few slaves in Connecticut at the time, and slavery there was not a pressing issue except to abolitionists and a few other groups. Many residents, however, clung to racist views that had developed during a long history of slave ownership in the state.

Originally the home of the Quinnipiack Native American tribe, New Haven became a Puritan outpost with the arrival of minister John Davenport and his followers in 1638. Davenport hoped to establish a Christian utopia on the shores of Long Island Sound. With him came a group of wealthy merchants intent on guaranteeing the commercial success of the venture. The Puritans, including Davenport, brought slaves with them to their new home. By the late 1830s, almost thirteen thousand people lived in the city. A major New England port and manufacturing center, New Haven had its own court-house, an impressive town square, and an arms factory established by Eli Whitney, inventor of the cotton gin.

Altogether, Connecticut residents owned four thousand slaves in 1755. But as the economy shifted to manufacturing and European immigrants began filling jobs, slaves played a less important role in the state's economy. Owning a slave—and supporting that slave for life—became more expensive than hiring a servant.

In 1784 Connecticut voters adopted a plan that would free slaves gradually over several decades. Under the "gradual emancipation" law, all slaves born before 1784 remained slaves for life. Those born after that date would be freed once they turned twenty-five (later, twenty-one). The law allowed slave owners to benefit from slaves' work while they were young and healthy and to avoid supporting them in old age.

The system eventually eliminated slavery in the state. By 1820 there were ninety-seven slaves in Connecticut and none by 1850. According to the 1840 census, conducted during the *Amistad* trials, 8,111 free blacks and fifty-four black slaves lived in Connecticut.

Many of the region's citizens were against slavery, but they did not support the abolitionists' efforts. Racists stirred up mobs and led them to violently oppose any attempts to better the lot of the area's black residents. In New Haven, abolitionists Arthur Tappan and the Rev. Simeon Jocelyn met overwhelming opposition to their proposal in 1831 for a college for blacks in the city. At a special town meeting called to address the issue, seven hundred city leaders voted against the proposal. New Haven lawyer Roger Sherman Baldwin was one of only four to support the black college. Among those opposing the measure was Ralph I. Ingersoll, former New Haven mayor and a member of the U.S. Congress. Ingersoll

HARTFORD, CONNECTICUT, THE STATE CAPITAL, AS VIEWED FROM THE EASTERN BANK OF THE CONNECTICUT RIVER. THE *AMISTAD* CAPTIVES WERE TAKEN TO CONNECTICUT, WHERE SLAVERY WAS STILL ALLOWED IN 1839. STATE COURTS IN HARTFORD HEARD THE *AMISTAD* CASE BEFORE IT WAS APPEALED TO THE U.S. SUPREME COURT.

served as lawyer for the Spanish Crown at the *Amistad* trials.

The day after the town meeting, a mob attacked Tappan's house and later that year destroyed homes in the city's black community. Three years later, another mob attacked Jocelyn's house. He eventually was forced to resign as minister of the local Congregational church.

Faced with such violent opposition, the abolitionists had to abandon efforts to establish the nation's first black college.

TALES OF MURDER AND PIRACY

The first reports of the *Amistad* affair in the local papers portrayed the Spaniards as victims of black "buccaneers." The article in the August 26 edition of the *New London Gazette* reported that the "chief of the buccaneers" had sentenced Montes to death the day before and that "the grim crew" had chanted his "death song" and brandished their sabers over "his devoted head."

The reporter described Cinque as the "master-spirit and hero of this bloody tragedy." The black leader, according to the account, had cut the throats of the captain and crew members, threatened to kill Montes, and whipped his fellow slaves to keep them under his control. Nevertheless, the reporter portrayed the young leader with grudging respect. Cinque, the newspaper reported, had an "unusually intelligent" face and displayed "uncommon decision and coolness, with a composure characteristic of true courage and nothing to mark him as a malicious man." He was put in chains and taken to the New Haven jail along with the other blacks aboard the *Amistad*.

Relying on Ruiz's version of events, the reporter wrote that the Spaniard—a "very gentlemanly and intelligent young man"—owned most of the slaves (all but the cabin boy) and much of the cargo aboard the *Amistad*. Ruiz spoke fluent English as well as Spanish. Montes spoke Spanish, and the black captives spoke in a foreign tongue that no one in the area could understand.

Ruiz claimed that he and Montes had bought the captives in Cuba, where slavery was legal. International law banned the buying and selling of blacks born free and enslaved by merchants of the slave trade. However, many

Caribbean nations, including Spanish-owned Cuba and southern states in the United States, allowed slavery and the buying and selling of slaves living in their territory.

According to the newspaper account, the vessel and the cargo, valued at $40,000, had been insured in Havana before the voyage. The reporter estimated the value of the slaves at between $20,000 and $30,000.

Ruiz and Montes were not the only ones to lay claim to *Amistad* "property." Vessels in danger at sea relied on help from nearby ships. Without such assistance, the entire ship, its crew, and its cargo would be lost. As a reward for saving a ship, the rescuers historically received a percentage of the value of what was salvaged. In the case of the *Amistad*, that included slaves. Lieutenant Thomas Gedney, the commander of the USS *Washington*, who had captured the Africans and ordered the *Amistad* towed to Connecticut, filed the first salvage claim. He asked for a hearing in district court on his claim in order to recover a reward for rescuing the badly damaged *Amistad* and its cargo. In making the claim, he included the blacks as part of the cargo to be salvaged.

Others lined up to get their share of the salvage from the ill-fated *Amistad*. Captain Henry Green, the man who met the group from the *Amistad* on a Long Island beach, claimed a percentage of the salvage value of the slaves. The heirs of Ramon Ferrer, the slain captain of the *Amistad*, made a claim to recover cabin boy Antonio, his personal slave. Cuban merchants, who owned part of the cargo, also filed claims.

On August 29, federal district judge for Connecticut Andrew T. Judson held an inquiry on board the USS *Washington*. Gedney and his crew presented the court with a detailed list of "a large & valuable Cargo." The invoice described such goods as "11 Boxes Crockery & Glassware," "200 Boxes vermacelli," and "800 yds Striped linen."

These items, along with the schooner and its fittings, were worth an estimated $40,000.

No one represented the slaves, who could not speak the language of their captors. The claimants regarded them as property. In Gedney's accounting of the cargo, he included "fifty four Slaves to wit fifty one male slaves and three young female slaves who were worth twenty five Thousand Dollars."

During the proceedings, Ruiz gave this account of the mutiny:

> In the night I heard a noise in the forecastle. All of us were asleep except the man at the helm. I saw this man Joseph Cinque. There was no moon. It was very dark. I took up an oar and tried to quell the mutiny; I cried no! no! Then I heard one of the crew cry murder. [The captives rushed the deck and seized the Spaniards.] They told me I should not be hurt. They tied our hands. The slaves told us next day they had killed all.

After listening to the testimony, Judge Judson divided the case between two courts. The salvage claims would remain in district court. The criminal aspects of the case, including murder and piracy charges, would be transferred to a grand jury, which would convene at U.S. Circuit Court in Hartford in September.

The judge also ordered that the blacks be held at the New Haven jail until the case was settled.

A cause célèbre for abolitionists

For the Africans, the day ended with a stroke of good luck. Dwight Janes, a New London abolitionist who attended the inquiry, asked Ruiz if the captives could speak Spanish. Ruiz reportedly said, "No, they were just from Africa."

LEWIS TAPPAN: INNOVATOR AND INSPIRATION

LEWIS TAPPAN, A PROMINENT BUSINESSMAN AND CHRISTIAN ABOLITIONIST, AIDED THE *AMISTAD* CAPTIVES AND PAID FOR THEIR DEFENSE.

Lewis Tappan, among the most courageous of the anti-slavery activists of his day, was a man of many contradictions. Born in Northampton, Massachusetts, in 1788, he went into business for himself, made poor investments, accepted only cash payments, and went bankrupt. He then joined his brother Arthur in his successful silk business in New York City, where he established the nation's first credit reporting service. The concept changed the way America did business and brought Tappan great wealth. The company he created eventually became Dun & Bradstreet, the largest credit reporting firm in the world today.

Tappan was an ardent Christian who helped inspire the first African missions of the American Missionary Association (which would become a branch of the United Church of Christ). He loved America, and hated slavery, which he called "the worm at the root of the tree of Liberty."

He, his brother Arthur, and Theodore Weld formed the American Anti-Slavery Society in 1833 and helped finance its newspaper, the *Emancipator*. A man of letters as well as figures, Lewis Tappan served as reporter for the *Emancipator*, attending the *Amistad* trials and filing reports each day.

Tappan relished a fight and seemed to thrive on the abuse he took. Outraged racists burned him in effigy and sent him hate mail and death threats. Someone once mailed a slave's ear to Tappan as a warning. Another unnamed enemy offered a $100,000 reward to anyone who killed the Tappan brothers and dumped their bodies in a slave state. When a mob incensed by the activities of Tappan's American Anti-Slavery Society trashed his home and burned his furniture in the street, Tappan wrote to Weld that he wanted his house to remain "this summer as it is, a silent anti-slavery preacher to the crowds who will see it."

Even many abolitionists found his views radical. He believed that intermarriage among the races—creating a "copper-colored" nation—would alleviate the racial divide that plagued America. An early proponent of education, Tappan and his brother helped pay for black schools and pushed for equal education for blacks. He won a victory when Oberlin College, to which he contributed large sums, became the first college in the United States to accept black students of both sexes.

For each advance, however, there was a setback. In one such battle, Tappan faced Connecticut District Court Judge Andrew T. Judson, who would later preside over the *Amistad* case. The judge opposed the efforts of a Quaker woman, Prudence Crandall, to open a school for black girls near Judson's Connecticut home. He convinced the state assembly to pass the "Connecticut Black Law" barring nonresident blacks from local schools. After Judson prosecuted Crandall, the first defendant under the new law, and obtained a conviction, the Tappans paid for her appeal. She won in court on a technicality, but closed her school after a mob ransacked her house.

The *Amistad* case appealed to Tappan from the beginning. He believed the Africans had been "brought by the providence of God," and he, more than anyone, made it his mission to help them. Throughout the Supreme Court hearings, Tappan's daughter Eliza lay bedridden from tuberculosis. She died two months after the *Amistad* captives won their case. Despite his grief, Tappan accompanied the Africans when they performed at New York City's Broadway Tabernacle a week after Eliza's death.

The Africans remained indebted to this man who had spent so much of his time and his money on their case. As Cinque neared home aboard the *Gentleman* in January 1842, the African leader wrote a letter to Tappan to express his gratitude and deep affection:

> Mr. Tappan—Dear sir: . . . All Mendi people love Mr. Tappan. Mr. Tappan, pray for Cinque and all Mendi people all time, and Cinque and all Mendi people pray for Mr. Tappan all time. . . . Cinque love Mr. Tappan very much, and all Mendi people love Mr. Tappan very much. I no forget Mr. Tappan forever and ever; and I no forget God, because God help Mr. Tappan for Mendi people. . . . I thank all 'merica people for they send Mendi people home. I shall never forget 'merica people.
> Your friend, CINQUE.

The comment, seemingly acknowledging that the captives had recently come from Africa, led the abolitionists to believe the slaves were not from Cuba after all. Instead, they surmised that the *Amistad* captives had been kidnapped in Africa and transported to Cuba illegally. A U.S. law passed in 1820 established that slave trading was piracy and set the death penalty for violators.

Janes contacted Joshua Leavitt, editor of the New York abolitionist newspaper the *Emancipator*, who in turn notified Lewis Tappan, a wealthy New York businessman and leading antislavery activist. Tappan had embraced the abolitionist cause. He had helped finance the campaign for a black university, which his brother Arthur had helped organize. In 1833 the two brothers, along with Theodore Weld, had formed the American Anti-Slavery Society and had established the *Emancipator* to report on abolitionist activities. After a mob damaged his home and burned his furniture in the street, Tappan ordered the smoldering remains to be left in place "as it is, a silent antislavery preacher to the crowds who will see it."

With Tappan involved, the plight of the Africans soon became a cause célèbre for the antislavery movement. He raised funds, organized a support committee, recruited a legal defense team, visited the Africans, agitated for better treatment, and even helped teach them English. Simeon S. Jocelyn, a noted abolitionist and white pastor of a black church in New York, and editor Leavitt joined Tappan on the Amistad Committee. Together they hired Baldwin, the antislavery lawyer who had been among the few to support Arthur Tappan's black college proposal. Theodore Sedgwick Jr. and Seth P. Staples assisted Baldwin in the defense.

In the days leading up to the first trial, scheduled for mid-September, Tappan's committee set about to change the public's perception of the black captives and modify press coverage of the events surrounding their case. In one of its first official acts, the committee issued a fundraising appeal for the Africans' defense. The ad, published in the *Commercial Advertiser* on September 5, portrayed the Africans as men worthy of sympathy. The ad read:

> Thirty-eight fellow-men from Africa, after having been piratically kidnapped from their native land, transported across the seas, and subjected to atrocious cruelties, have been thrown upon our shores, and are now incarcerated in jail to await their trial for crimes alleged by their oppressors to have been committed by them. They are ignorant of our language, of the usages of civilized society, and the obligations of christianity.

The blatantly proslavery newspaper the *New York Morning Herald* also recognized the publicity value of the incident to the abolitionists. "The affair of the *Amistad*," the paper reported in its September 17 edition, "is a godsend to these men." The report described the abolitionists as "infatuated and mischievous men" who were working hard to produce "a fatal schism between the free states and the slave states."

Newspaper accounts and circulars focused attention on Cinque, the young leader of the captives. A man who examined Cinque's skull to determine his characteristics—a pseudoscience called phrenology that was popular in the 1800s—issued a scholarly report on his conclusions. The phrenologist, who measured Cinque's skull during a visit to his New Haven jail cell, painted a favorable portrait of the African leader. He saw Cinque as a man with "a love of liberty, independence, determination, ambition, regard for his country, and for what he thinks is sacred and right; also, good practical talents and powers of observation, shrewdness, tact, and management, joined with an uncommon degree of moral courage and pride of character."

Other articles, however, were far less complimentary. The *New York Morning Herald* described Cinque as "a sullen, dumpish looking negro, with a flat nose, thick lips, and all the other characteristics of his debased countrymen, without a single redeeming or striking trait, except the mere brute qualities of strength and activity."

A minstrel show performing at the Bowery Theater in New York during that time borrowed its theme from the *Amistad* case. The playbill advertising the show trumpeted, "Piracy! mutiny! & murder!"

An International Affair

The matter became an international affair when Spain entered the fray on behalf of its citizens. On September 6, Angel Calderon de la Barca, Spain's minister to the United States, wrote to U.S. Secretary of State John Forsyth to demand the return of the *Amistad* and its cargo to the Spanish citizens who claimed them. In addition, he demanded that the slaves be sent to Havana to be tried on piracy and murder charges by a Spanish court. U.S. courts, he argued, had no jurisdiction in the case.

The Spanish minister cited four articles of Pinckney's Treaty of 1795, which had been written to stabilize relations between Spain and the United States. Under Pinckney's Treaty, negotiated by Thomas Pinckney, each nation pledged to provide a safe haven to vessels owned by citizens of the other nation whenever the ships were "forced through stress of weather, pursuit of Pirates or Enemies, or any other urgent necessity" to seek shelter. The treaty also stipulated that vessels rescued from pirates or robbers should be taken into custody until the proper

PRESIDENT MARTIN VAN BUREN WAS IN THE MIDST OF A TOUGH REELECTION CAMPAIGN WHEN THE *AMISTAD* INCIDENT OCCURRED. HE FEARED SOUTHERN VOTERS WOULD RESENT ANY ACTION TO FREE THE CAPTIVES.

owners could produce documents to prove their claim. Once that had been done, according to the treaty, the vessels—Spanish or American—would be released to the owners.

The Adams–Onís Treaty of 1819, signed by Spanish

foreign minister Louis de Onís and U.S. Secretary of State John Quincy Adams, reaffirmed the terms of the Pinckney Treaty. It became effective in 1831.

In his letter to Forsyth, the Spanish minister called upon "the law of nations, the stipulations of existing treaties, and those good feelings so necessary to the maintenance of the friendly relations that subsist between the two countries and are so interesting to both." He demanded that the *Amistad* and all its cargo be returned to its Spanish owners without any amount being paid for salvage costs. In addition, he maintained that no U.S. court had the right to consider the case because it involved a Spanish vessel and Spanish citizens.

U.S. President Martin Van Buren, in the midst of a heated reelection campaign, had no wish to deal with an international dispute, especially one that threatened to kindle the smoldering controversy over slavery. In fact, the incident could not have come at a worse time for the embattled president. A skilled politician who helped build the Democratic Party, Van Buren succeeded Andrew Jackson after serving as vice president. Soon after he took office, however, the economy slumped into a depression and border disputes increased tensions with Great Britain and Spain. His opposition to annexing Texas helped keep peace with Spain. Southerners, however, wanted Texas to join the union as a slave state to bolster their side in the slavery dispute. Van Buren came from a New York family that had owned slaves, and he himself had had a slave when he was a young man. Despite these credentials and the fact that the Democratic Party had dominated Southern politics, the South viewed the president with suspicion. To bolster support from the South, the Democrats issued the first party platform. In it, they rejected the abolition of slavery and endorsed a provision that would prevent debate on the issue.

WILLIAM HENRY HARRISON, THE WHIG CANDIDATE FOR U.S. PRESIDENT, WAGED A BRUTAL CAMPAIGN AGAINST PRESIDENT MARTIN VAN BUREN. HARRISON WON THE ELECTION, BUT HE DIED OF PNEUMONIA WITHIN A MONTH OF TAKING OFFICE.

William Henry Harrison, Whig candidate for president, threatened to unseat Van Buren in his bid for reelection. The Whigs—who had already tagged the president "Martin Van Ruin"—had embarked on a fierce campaign to discredit their opponent. They used the economy and Van Buren's stance on Texas to undermine support for the president.

Founded around 1834 to counter Andrew Jackson and his Democratic Party, the Whig Party opposed a strong presidency, favoring instead a powerful Congress. The Whigs pushed for economic development and focused on improvements to roads, railways, and other infrastructure. The debate over the expansion of slavery to western territories split the party, and it disbanded in 1856.

The Harrison campaign billed its candidate as a war hero and common man, even though he belonged to an elite Virginia family. Harrison supporters staged rousing partisan events, marching in parades and wheeling floats of log cabins and cider barrels. The Democrats had made the mistake, earlier in the campaign, of ridiculing Harrison as a country bumpkin. "Give him a barrel of hard [alcoholic] cider and settle a pension of two thousand a year on him, and take my word for it, he will sit the remainder of his days in his log cabin," a partisan newspaper had written. The Whigs used the insult to good advantage by portraying their candidate as a man of the people, while painting Van Buren as a stuffed shirt.

Both Harrison and his vice presidential running mate, John Tyler, came from Virginia, a fact that the Whigs hoped would bring them support from the South. Harrison owned slaves and supported the right of states to decide the slavery issue for themselves. Van Buren feared that Harrison and his supporters would use the *Amistad* case to turn the South against him.

To prevent that, the president intended to deliver the

black captives, the vessel, and its contents to the Spanish government as quickly as possible. Until the court ruled in the case, however, the captives would remain at the New Haven jail.

TWO
SLAVERY AND THE SLAVE TRADE

THE FIRST AFRICAN SLAVES stepped foot on North American soil not long after the Jamestown colonists arrived in 1607. A Dutch ship, after sailing through a rough storm off the coast of Virginia, landed at the colony in 1619. Low on supplies, the ship's captain traded about twenty slaves on board for food. The slaves, originally captured in Africa by a Spanish crew, had been seized by the Dutch. Portuguese, Spanish, British, and other Europeans had kidnapped and enslaved Africans for more than a century before this, bringing most of the slaves to colonies in South and Central America to work the plantations.

In the 1500s Europeans enslaved the native populations in the Caribbean nations of Jamaica, Haiti, and Cuba to work on sugar plantations and other agricultural operations. After the native peoples died out in large numbers, the Europeans shipped in African slaves to do the work.

Historians dispute whether the Africans brought to Jamestown were treated as slaves—captive for life—or indentured servants, who earned their freedom and a small plot of land by working for a number of years for the English colonists. Blacks as well as whites seem to have followed this route to freedom in the early colonies, according to census records. They married, had children, and owned property.

There is no doubt, however, that some Africans remained enslaved for life. A court in colonial Virginia decreed in 1640, for example, that a runaway African worker would "serve his said master or his assigns for the time of his natural life here or elsewhere."

In other cases, Virginia courts ruled in favor of blacks. In a 1641 case, for example, the court allowed a black man to buy his child's freedom even though the mother was a slave. He promised to raise the child in the Christian faith. Another case involved a black servant who had been promised his freedom after working eight years. After three more years of enforced servitude, he appealed to the court, which released him.

A system that freed workers, however, threatened the colonial farmers' success. To harvest the large tobacco fields in Virginia, they needed a large and permanent labor force. Slavery, relying on captives from Africa, soon filled that need.

The Portuguese first enslaved Africans in 1441. The traders discovered that slaves could bring more profit than the gold they originally sought in Africa. They set up trade with Africans, who brought in slaves in return for guns, iron, cloth, and other goods from Europe. By the time Columbus sighted land in the Caribbean Sea, slave traders had delivered almost two hundred thousand African captives to Europe. With the development of North and South America came a rapid increase in the demand for slave labor. By the early 1600s the Spanish and Portuguese colonies in South and Central America had imported a million African slaves to work on the region's massive sugar plantations.

Britain's North American colonies turned to slave labor in the 1600s and 1700s to work the cotton, tobacco, and rice plantations in the South and supply labor on family farms and in households in the North. During

AFRICAN MEN, WOMEN, AND CHILDREN, CAPTURED IN THEIR HOMELAND,
WERE SOLD AS SLAVES TO LANDOWNERS IN NORTH AMERICA.

more than three centuries, European slave ships brought 10 to 12 million African slaves to the Americas.

A Lucrative Trade

The trade became a lucrative source of income for merchants of many nations, including Britain and its American colonies. Participating in what was referred to as a "golden triangle," slave traders transported goods from the Americas to Europe, where they traded the goods for guns and other merchandise. They then traded these items for African slaves, whom they transported to the Americas in exchange for more goods. All along the triangle's route, merchants raked in gold for their efforts. In Rhode Island, for example, slave traders bought rum, which they transported to Africa and traded for slaves. The slaves, in turn, were traded for Caribbean molasses and sugar, which the merchants transported to Rhode Island to be used to make more rum.

The slave trade severely damaged African society. White slave traders were not allowed into Africa's interior. They depended on Africans to bring them captives, for which the traders paid them in guns, alcohol, iron, and other goods. This pitted one community against another and encouraged kidnappings and attacks on neighboring tribes. The influx of guns increased warfare and violence. Many promising young leaders disappeared, captured and shipped to America as slaves. Most came from among the Mendi, the Kisi, the Kono, and other inland peoples.

Not all slaves were kidnapped or captured. Some were serving as slaves to pay off debts and were sold to the traders. They joined the other captives on the long walk—for some as much as one thousand miles—across Africa to huge forts that housed thousands of slaves. These slave factories, built on the coast of western Africa, held the captives until they could be shipped to overseas markets.

The *Amistad* slaves had been held in one such factory, on an island called Lomboko in the Gallinas River delta. Don Pedro Blanco, a notorious Spanish slave merchant who controlled a large portion of the trade, ran the Lomboko factory. Associates described him as living in "a semi-barbarous manner, at once, as a private gentleman and an African prince."

According to reports of the day, Blanco ran a businesslike operation that extended from Africa to the Caribbean and the United States. He relied on a network of corrupt black mercenary chiefs who organized kidnapping forays in inner Africa. Branch offices in Havana and representatives in Puerto Rico, Trinidad, and Texas handled sales in the Americas. Blanco also ran a legitimate trading business with clients worldwide. Major banks in New York, London, and other financial centers provided financing. One visitor to Lomboko, marveling at the immensity of the operation, described it as "not only the centre of an extensive and lucrative traffic, but the theatre of a new order of society and a novel form of government." Reportedly, slave ships transported two thousand slaves a year from the Gallinas River delta to markets in the Americas.

Gruesome passage

After being held for up to a year in the factories' underground prisons, slaves then had to face the "Middle Passage," the gruesome and often deadly journey aboard the slave ships to America. The traders crammed men, women, and children into the ship's hold, three hundred to four hundred in an area with little or no headroom. Chains bound them together in the dark hold. Many ships stowed their human cargo on two levels, in a space too shallow to allow a person to sit up. When the weather was rough, they slid across the floor from side to side. The ship's unventilated hold reeked with human waste, perspiration, and the vile odor of those who had died.

A passage by an unidentified writer in the Congo in 1859 described the horror of the experience:

> Now their sufferings become dreadful—horrible; indeed, human language is incapable of describing, or imagination of sketching even the faint outline of a dimly floating fancy of what their condition is— homesick, seasick, half starved, naked, crying for air, for water, the strong killing the weak or dying in order to make room, the hold becomes a perfect charnel house of death and misery—a misery and anguish only conceivable by those who have endured it.

A normal crossing took two to three months. In bad weather, however, ships could take up to four months to cross the Atlantic. Slaves were valuable commodities, so traders tried to keep them alive during the passage. Nevertheless, an estimated 10 to 20 percent died during the crossing. Because insurance companies typically did not pay for slaves who died from disease but would cover those who drowned, some captains threw sick captives overboard.

Cuba, a Spanish territory, served as a major port for the slave trade. Merchants gathered at the slave markets in Havana and other Cuban ports to bid on the offerings from Africa as well as local sources. According to census records, Cuba had a slave population of 287,000 in 1827. Once purchased, the captives were taken to plantations in the Caribbean and the U.S. South and other locales, where they and their offspring would be enslaved for life. Under Cuban law, slaves could buy their freedom and many did, increasing the black and mixed-race population of the island.

American Slave Traders

In 1644 Boston traders entered the lucrative slave trade by seizing West Africans and selling them in the West Indies. In the 1670s Massachusetts shippers sold captives from Madagascar to Virginia plantation owners. They also sold slaves in Connecticut and Rhode Island. The American trade was limited at first by the big cartels that controlled most of the slave business. By the early 1700s the English had become masters of the seas, which opened the slave trade to American merchants.

In 1641 Massachusetts became the first American colony to legalize slavery when the legislature passed regulations governing slaves. According to the Puritans, the Bible authorized slavery, and the regulations followed the moral code of "the law of God, established in Israel concerning such people." The Puritans believed slavery was "punishment" for a race of people described by renowned Boston Puritan minister Cotton Mather as the "miserable children of Adam and Noah."

Other colonies followed suit. In 1670 Virginia lawmakers decreed that all non-Christian blacks brought into the state would be slaves for life. By then, about two thousand blacks lived in the colony, most of whom worked on the big plantations. Another law, passed in 1705, made *all* blacks in Virginia lifelong slaves. By then, ten thousand blacks lived in Virginia, about one-fifth of the colony's population. In 1750 Georgia became the last of the British colonies in America to make slavery legal.

Declaring their independence from British control, the colonists affirmed their belief that "all men are created equal." But after winning the Revolutionary War, they clarified that such equality did not extend to slaves. Several founders, including George Washington and Thomas Jefferson, the author of the Declaration of Independence, owned slaves. Northerners, with few slaves, did not want slaves considered at all when doling out Congressional seats. As a compromise between southern and northern states, the founders included a provision in the new constitution that counted slaves as three-fifths of a person when determining the number of representatives to Congress allotted each state. The same formula was used to figure taxation.

Congress also passed a law that barred future law-makers from prohibiting the importation of slaves until 1808. The law guaranteed that the slave trade bringing Africans to the United States would be permitted for the next twenty years.

PUSH TO END SLAVE TRADE

At the same time, however, groups in America and England were pushing to abolish slavery and end the slave trade. The Quakers, among others, opposed the practice in England and America and won converts with their speeches and writings. In 1772 the English chief justice ruled against slavery, a decision that would eventually lead to freedom for England's fifteen thousand slaves. Bloody uprisings among slaves in British territories also helped turn the public's sentiments against slavery and the cruel slave trade that fed the system. In 1807 England abolished the slave trade, banning vessels flying the British flag from participating in the slave business. That year, too, Congress made it illegal to import slaves into the United States. The law, however, did not take effect until 1808.

By 1815 Russia, Austria, Prussia, France, the Netherlands, Sweden, and the United States had joined England in barring their ships from the slave trade. Two years later Spain banned its vessels from trading in slaves north of the equator. In 1820 Spanish ships were prohibited from the slave trade altogether. By 1839, the year

AN ENGRAVING DEPICTS MEN ON HORSEBACK WHIPPING SLAVES BEING TAKEN
TO BE SOLD AT A SLAVE MARKET IN THE SOUTH. ALTHOUGH THE UNITED
STATES SIGNED A TREATY BANNING THE INTERNATIONAL SLAVE TRADE,
SELLING OF SLAVES WITHIN THE COUNTRY WAS ALLOWED.

Amistad set out on its fateful journey, slave trafficking was illegal everywhere in the world.

Despite the international bans, however, the lucrative slave trade continued almost unabated. Demand for slaves—and therefore, prices—remained high. Traders could make a huge return, paying as little as $20 for an African slave they could sell in Cuba's slave markets for $350. Although the United States prohibited the slave trade, it, like many other nations, continued to support slavery. The United States also permitted the buying and selling of slaves already in the Americas; only the importation of African slaves fell under the ban. Using that loophole, traders disguised the origins of the African captives they sold as slaves in America.

In 1808 Great Britain became the international enforcer of the ban on the slave trade. Treaties with several other nations that declared slave trading as piracy gave England the right to search vessels and seize those suspected of trading in slaves. Americans wary of British power refused to allow their old enemy to board U.S. ships. The enmity between the two powers increased when a British ship rammed the USS *Chesapeake* and forced the sailors to serve in the British navy. Taking advantage of the situation, many slave traders flew U.S. flags to avoid capture by the British patrol. Not until 1862 did the United States agree to sign a treaty that allowed British officers to board suspicious U.S. vessels.

Britain established a base of operations in Sierra Leone, in western Africa. A deadly cat-and-mouse game ensued. Anchored just out of sight of the British patrols, slave ships waited for lookouts perched in trees to signal them close to shore. Those on land loaded slaves into canoes and ferried them to the waiting vessels, quickly transferring them to the hold and then slipping quietly away. It took only two hours to board two hundred slaves.

By the mid-1830s Britain had more than fifteen vessels assigned to the antislavery fleet. The effort helped deter some traders, but many others managed to elude the British, transporting an estimated 2.7 million slaves from Africa to Cuba and other American ports between 1807 and 1860. During that time British ships confiscated 1,600 ships involved in the slave trade and released 150,000 African captives.

A BRUTAL BUSINESS

Beginning in the 1820s and early 1830s, nations throughout the world began turning away from slavery. Few could deny that slavery was a brutal business, enforced by whips and chains and punctuated by bloody uprisings. The public's outrage flared with each new violent explosion. A slave revolt in Santo Domingo in 1791 spread like wildfire and eventually led to Haiti's independence and the end of slavery in French colonies. An aborted revolt in Richmond, Virginia, ended with the hanging of thirty-six slaves in 1800. U.S. troops had to respond to several slave revolts in the 1810s and 1820s, resulting in many deaths. Nat Turner, a slave in Virginia, led the most famous uprising in 1831. Three thousand state militiamen crushed the rebellion, which had involved only about fifty or sixty slaves. Fifty whites died in the battle and more than one hundred slaves were killed in retribution. Turner, captured six weeks later, was executed.

By the mid-1830s the peoples of Central America, Chile, Mexico, and Bolivia had ended slavery in their lands. Six years before the *Amistad* incident, in 1833, Great Britain abolished slavery in all its colonies.

The United States, nonetheless, continued its support of slavery. The issue, however, created a wedge between Southerners, who depended on slave labor to work their plantations, and Northerners, who had far fewer slaves and an economy that did not rely on slavery. As early as 1777, Vermont became the first state to ban slavery in its constitution. Three years later Massachusetts included a similar provision in its state constitution. Several other northern states, including Connecticut, adopted provisions to phase out slavery gradually.

For decades the North accepted what they called the South's "peculiar institution." In 1818 the nation's twenty-two states were evenly divided between eleven states that allowed slavery and eleven states that did not. But as settlers began pushing to set up their own states, the slavery issue became more divisive. In 1820, after a long, contentious battle in the Senate, the U.S. Congress agreed to the Missouri Compromise, which conferred statehood on Missouri, where slavery was allowed, and on Maine, where slavery was not allowed, thus maintaining the balance between free and slave states.

The controversy further emphasized the divide between the North and the South. During the debate on the matter, U.S. Representative Arthur Livermore from New Hampshire asked his fellow legislators, "How long will the desire for wealth render us blind to the sin of holding both the bodies and souls of our fellow men in chains?"

His comments reflected the growing opposition to slavery among some Northern activists. These antislavery advocates were called abolitionists because they called for slavery to be abolished everywhere. Abolitionist groups in the North helped runaway slaves escape from their masters and pushed politicians to support their cause. The movement would later grow out of a massive religious revival of the 1820s called the Second Great Awakening. The religious revival inspired New Englanders, in particular, to become involved in a variety of social crusades, among them abolition, women's rights, and prohibition of alcohol.

In 1831 William Lloyd Garrison launched the *Liberator*, a newspaper dedicated to the abolitionist cause. "I will be as harsh as truth and as uncompromising as justice," he declared in the first issue. "On this subject I do not wish to think or speak or write with moderation."

Garrison, brothers Arthur and Lewis Tappan, and sixty other delegates founded the American Anti-Slavery Society in 1833. Its mission, touted by the men and women of both races gathered in Philadelphia for the first meeting, was to abolish slavery.

The abolitionists' strident demands provoked the ire of Northerners as well as Southerners. Many Northerners, while not involved directly in slavery, benefited from trade dependent on slaves. Northern factories manufactured cotton goods; banks in the North financed tobacco and sugar plantations.

Abolitionists who dared to take a public stand against slavery often found themselves vilified, and sometimes attacked, by their own neighbors. In 1837 a mob of slave owners in Alton, Illinois, killed abolitionist editor Elijah P. Lovejoy during an attack aimed at destroying his printing press. A year later, another mob burned down Pennsylvania Hall in Philadelphia to prevent abolitionists from meeting there. Officials blamed abolitionists for inciting the violent attack.

Even people opposed to slavery feared that abolishing it would damage the nation's economy and lead to violence, perhaps even war. By the late 1830s the abolitionist movement had split into factions. They disagreed over women's participation in the campaign, the role of blacks, how to deal with politics, and the part to be played by churches. Garrison, for one, held harsh views on politics. He urged followers not to vote or join a political party and

A MOB CHARGES THE HOUSE OF ELIJAH LOVEJOY, EDITOR AND ABOLITIONIST, IN ALTON, ILLINOIS. THE ANGRY CROWD KILLED THE NEWSPAPERMAN IN THE 1837 ATTACK. LOVEJOY'S ANTISLAVERY ARTICLES INFURIATED SLAVEHOLDERS.

even argued for the dissolution of the union. He viewed the Constitution as a "covenant with death."

This was the atmosphere, simmering with controversy, as *Amistad* and its African captives reached Long Island Sound and sailed into American history.

THREE
CLAIMS AGAINST THE *AMISTAD*

THE arrival OF THE Africans aboard the *Amistad* was the most exciting event to occur in Connecticut in decades. "These blacks have created a greater excitement in Connecticut than any event there since the close of the last century," an article in the *New York Herald* reported.

The Africans had been taken to New Haven's county jail while awaiting trial. They wore cotton shirts and trousers provided by U.S. Marshal Norris Willcox. A local doctor had examined them and treated those who were ill.

Officials used the Africans' notoriety to good advantage. The jailer collected a New York shilling (about twelve cents) apiece from the four or five thousand people who lined up each day to view the black men and children from Africa. The Africans put on a good show, turning somersaults and leaping about the green, where the jailer had taken them to exercise. According to a newspaper report, the money collected would be used for the Africans' benefit after paying the jailer "a just compensation for his trouble."

Throughout this time, as controversy swirled around them, the Africans remained an enigma, unable to tell their side of the story. They could not communicate with the lawyers or the members of the committee formed to help them. Joshua Leavitt and Lewis Tappan brought natives of Africa to the jail, hoping they might be able to

THE REV. THOMAS GALLAUDET, A RENOWNED LINGUIST AND LEADER IN EDU-
CATING THE DEAF, HAD SOME SUCCESS COMMUNICATING WITH THE *AMISTAD*
CAPTIVES USING SIGN LANGUAGE.

understand the captives' language. Since the *Amistad*
Africans came from a different part of that continent,
however, they could not understand the black men any
better than their white companions.

As the trial approached, the *Amistad* lawyers tried
desperately to find someone who could talk with their
clients. One captive, Bahoo, could speak a smattering of
English, but not enough to be of much use to the defense.

At one point the lawyers brought in Thomas Gallaudet, a linguist who founded the American School for the Deaf in Hartford, the first permanent school for deaf children in the United States. Gallaudet was renowned for his work with the deaf and his use of sign language. (Gallaudet's son, Edward Miner Gallaudet, became the first superintendent of what became Gallaudet University in Washington, D.C., the first college specifically for the deaf.) After communicating with the Africans through sign language, Gallaudet reported that "they are, almost without exception, quick in their movement, animated in conversation, and, so far as can be judged by those who do not understand their language, they have intellects quite as acute as those of our Indians, or of any uncivilized people."

someone to talk to

Around this time, Lewis Tappan brought three native Africans to the jail. He hoped they would be able to serve as interpreters. Two other Africans joined them there. Of the five, only one, John Ferry, could understand anything the captives said. Because each village or district in Africa had its own dialect, even someone with a general knowledge of the language had a difficult time understanding a speaker from another region.

Ferry had been born in western Africa in a region about a day's journey south of Sierra Leone. Slave traders had kidnapped him when he was twelve and taken him to South America. He had been freed in Colombia. Ferry could speak and understand some words of Mandingo, spoken by a majority of the captives. A few of the jailed Africans spoke Gallina, another dialect of western Africa that Ferry could understand and speak more fluently.

The captives were jubilant when Ferry spoke words they knew. "You may imagine the joy manifested by these poor

Africans," Tappan wrote in a letter dated September 9, "when they heard one of their own color address them in a friendly manner, and in a language they could comprehend!" None of them, however, spoke Ferry's native dialect. Nevertheless, Ferry did his best to unravel the mystery of the Africans' saga.

Most of the captives, including two of the girls and the young boy, were from the Mandingo region in and around Sierra Leone in western Africa. A few others, including one of the girls, were from the Congo. Cinque told Ferry that he had been kidnapped and taken to Spanish slave traders in western Africa. They put him aboard a ship, where he met the other Africans who were now in the jail. A month and a half later, they landed in Havana. After a brief stay, they were taken aboard the *Amistad*, where the captain "beat them severely," according to Cinque.

The Africans decided to take over the ship. He recounted how the Spaniards deceived them by steering the boat westward during the night. They had no idea where they were when they sighted land. Cinque had led a scouting party ashore, where they met captains Fordham and Green and their men. Bahoo asked in broken English where they were. When Green told them they had landed in America, Bahoo asked if it was a slave country. Green had replied that it was free and safe.

Cinque told how he had given Green his saber, gun, and hat, hoping that the man would take them to Sierra Leone. Lieutenant Gedney blocked that plan when he took over the *Amistad* and apprehended Cinque and the rest of the Africans.

During a later session, Cinque told Tappan (through the interpreter) that his parents, wife, and three children had been left behind in Africa. He had been seized by African traders and sold to white slavers. Tappan said Cinque "drew his hand across his throat" and asked if the

Americans intended to kill him. When he assured Cinque that the Americans were his friends and would help him get back home, "his countenance immediately lost the anxious and distressed expression it had before, and beamed with joy." Tappan often went to the jail to instruct the Africans, especially the children, in the English language and Christianity.

UNTANGLING LEGAL KNOTS

On Tuesday, September 17, 1839, the Hartford court convened a grand jury to look into the *Amistad* case. The following day, the *Amistad* lawyers asked the circuit court judge in Hartford to release the three black girls, since they had not been charged with any crime. The judge agreed to hear the lawyers' arguments on the matter the next day in court when the entire *Amistad* case would be considered.

On September 19, 1839, two federal judges and a grand jury assembled in Hartford to try to untangle the legal knots posed in the *Amistad* case. The circuit court handled most federal criminal cases and some appeals, while the district court oversaw trials and settled admiralty law (governing maritime commerce and trade laws). Because the *Amistad* case involved criminal charges as well as admiralty law, the matter would have to be addressed in both courts. In addition, the grand jury conducted a separate review of the murder charges.

A crowd gathered in front of Hartford's brick courthouse long before the trial's appointed hour. Hotel rooms were filled to capacity with visiting lawyers, reporters, and others eager to get a front-row seat for the proceedings. Outside the two-story courthouse, a party atmosphere pervaded the late-summer day. People ate from picnic lunches on the courthouse lawn. Street vendors sold *Amistad* memorabilia to the curious crowds. All eyes turned to the Connecticut River, where a parade of boats carried the participants to trial. Spaniards Ruiz and Montes and Lieutenant Gedney arrived aboard a paddle steamboat. The Africans rode on a canal boat.

Judge Andrew T. Judson opened proceedings in the district court to hear the claims filed in the case. Having Judson, a well-known antiabolitionist, preside over the case did not bode well for the Africans or their abolitionist supporters. In ruling on an earlier case, Judson had observed that the United States was "a nation of white men and every American should indulge that pride and honor, which is falsely called prejudice, and teach it to his children. Nothing else will preserve the American name, or the American character. Who of you would like to see the glory of this nation stripped away, and given to another race of men?"

During the proceedings, a long line of claimants reeled off the property they sought. Ruiz and Montes claimed the slaves, while Gedney sought to collect fees for salvaging the vessel, and Green asked for payment for returning the slaves. The Spanish consul, represented by attorney Ralph Ingersoll, also asked to file a claim on behalf of the Spanish owner of the vessel, Jose Antonio Tellincas.

The final plea of the morning, presented by William Holabird, the U.S. Attorney for Connecticut, asked the court to end the proceedings as quickly as possible and deliver the Africans to the president, who would then turn them over to the Spanish government. Holabird cited the Act of 1819, which he claimed obligated the United States to return a foreign country's property.

In the claims that had been filed, the blacks were viewed as part of the property to be parceled out. At the end of the morning's session, however, Judge Judson, a Van Buren appointee, made an unexpected ruling. He announced that the court would not allow the Africans to be included in the claims for salvage. According to a newspaper report, the ruling was based on the grounds "that only property could be liable for salvage, and that these men could not be regarded in this State as property."

Born Free

During the afternoon session, *Amistad* lawyer Roger Baldwin asked for the release of the young African girls. The three girls, all under the age of eleven, were "brought into Court weeping, and evidently much terrified at the separation from their companions," according to an account of the proceedings. John Ferry, the interpreter, filed an affidavit with the court that the girls spoke the Gallina language "and no other." That fact and the girls' appearance proved to him that they were from Africa, not Cuba as claimed. With Ferry's help, Bahoo, the captive who understood some English, also swore in an affidavit that the girls and the young boy had come from Africa. Two of the girls were born in the Mandingo region of western Africa, in the same town he was from, Bahoo stated. In his affidavit, Bahoo also described the crossing from Africa to Havana:

> Good many in vessel, and many died—were tight together, two and two chained together by hands and feet, night and day, until near Havana, when the chains were taken off—were landed on the coast at a little place, near sun set—staid until night and walked into the city, put them into an old building and fastened them in—after some time the people now in jail [the *Amistad* Africans] were put on board the same vessel they came here in, in the night, and sailed away.

CHILDREN OF THE *AMISTAD*

Four children were aboard the *Amistad* when it sailed into Long Island Sound in 1839. The three little girls, Margru, Teme, and Kagne, and one boy, Kale, were all ten years old or younger when they arrived in America.

Like the men aboard the *Amistad*, the children had been kidnapped by slave traders in Africa and were forced to walk many miles to a slave factory on Lomboko Island. There, the traders crammed them into a dungeon with hundreds of other slaves. Eventually they boarded a Portuguese slave ship that took them to Havana, Cuba. During the months-long crossing, the children had to stay below deck with the African men, who had been stripped naked, chained, and forced to crouch in the hold.

Kale had been kidnapped as he walked down the street in his village. A gang of men grabbed Teme from her mother's house in the middle of the night. The families of Kagne and Margru sold them to pay off debts.

Margru, whose name meant "black snake" in her language, was born around 1832 in Mendi territory in western Africa. When she was six or seven, her family sold her to slave traders to pay off a debt. According to the records of a phrenologist who examined her before the *Amistad* trials, Margru stood four feet three inches tall. A sketch drawn by a New Haven portrait artist shows her to have had a high forehead, dark eyes, and a cautious smile. The Christian abolitionists who taught her religious lessons called her "the child of many prayers."

In a letter written September 9, 1839, Lewis Tappan described the children as "robust" and "full of hilarity." He said the sheriff had taken the children for a ride in a wagon. "At first their eyes were filled with tears, and they seemed to be afraid, but soon they enjoyed themselves very well, and appeared to be greatly delighted."

The girls dressed in calico frocks, brought to them by supporters of the Africans. They wrapped the little shawls they had also been given around their heads, like turbans. According to Tappan, the Africans looked at the clothes and "laughed a good deal among themselves" before putting them on.

At first the children spoke in their own dialects. One of the girls had come from the Congo and spoke a different language from the other three, who were Mendi. Under the tutelage of Tappan and others, the children began to learn to read and write English.

LITTLE KALE, THE ONLY YOUNG BOY ABOARD THE *AMISTAD*, WAS TEN YEARS OLD WHEN HE WAS CAPTURED AND TAKEN TO AMERICA.

Bright and eager to learn, the children memorized prayers translated by James Covey, the British sailor who served as the Africans' interpreter. Kale, the young boy, learned his lessons rapidly. He wrote a letter describing the children's studies:

We talk American language a little,
not very good. We write every-day;
we write plenty letters; we
read most all time; we read all
Matthew and Mark and Luke and
John, and plenty of little books. We
love books very much.

When the circuit court judge denied the petition to release the children, Tappan arranged for them to stay with the jailer and his wife in their home. As part of the deal, the girls worked as the family's servants.

The children moved with the other Africans to a farm in Farmington, Connecticut, after the U.S. Supreme Court ruling set them free. To raise money for the return trip to Africa, the group toured New York and New England, reading and writing Bible passages in English, performing skits about the *Amistad*, and singing. Kale and Margru were among the stars in the show. During this time the Christian abolitionists gave the girls American names: Teme became Maria, Kagne was renamed Charlotte, and Margru adopted the name Sarah Kinson. Tappan, however, later encouraged her to keep her African name as a good example to others. Sarah refused, saying that Margru was a heathen name.

In 1842 the children returned with the rest of their countrymen to Africa. Before they left, the freed captives of the *Amistad* sent John Quincy Adams a Bible to express their gratitude for his efforts on their behalf. Kale, probably the best writer in the group, wrote the letter of thanks that accompanied the gift.

On the return trip, the children occupied a stateroom with missionaries who planned on setting up a Christian outpost in western Africa. Once in Africa, they settled into their new lives at the Komende mission. Kale lived and worked at the mission and eventually married. As a young man, he fell ill with a disease that left him crippled for life. The girls also worked at the mission, Sarah as housekeeper, Charlotte as cook, and Maria as a housemaid. Sarah converted to Christianity. William Raymond, head of the mission, wrote to Tappan to urge him to arrange for Sarah to go to America to further her education. At age fourteen, Sarah returned to the United States, where Tappan arranged for her to live with an Oberlin College professor and attend the college. Oberlin had been the first college in the country to accept black students—under pressure from Tappan, who was a big donor.

While Sarah was at Oberlin, Charlotte, her *Amistad* shipmate, died from malaria. William Raymond also died from the disease. In 1849 Sarah returned to Africa, married, and with her husband taught at the mission. She later wrote to Tappan that she had found her father "living a good distance from the Mission." After her husband was fired from his mission post for "intemperance," Sarah seems to have disappeared from view, though there are reports that a school was named after her in Sierra Leone.

Little is known of Maria (Teme), other than that she lived and worked at the mission in Sierra Leone.

The judge deferred a decision on the children's case until the following day. A separate case held the attention of the judges for the remainder of the day.

The *Amistad* lawyers opened Friday's session with an appeal to set the Africans free. Attorney Theodore Sedgwick Jr. began by reading Spain's decree against the slave trade. He noted that the Africans had been born free and had a right to remain so. Defense lawyers argued that the Africans' kidnapping and illegal enslavement, not the killing of the crew, was the real crime. The deaths they caused by their mutiny "were incited by the love of liberty natural to all men."

Attorney Baldwin followed with an "elaborate argument" debunking the claims filed in the case, according to a report in the *New York Morning Herald*. Baldwin charged that the Africans had been illegally brought into Cuba and because of that, Montes, Ruiz, and the Spanish government had no claim on them. "No power on earth has the right to reduce [the Africans] to slavery," and the United States should never stoop so low as to become a "slave-catcher for foreign slave-holders," Baldwin argued.

Ingersoll countered, stating that the 1795 treaty with Spain gave that nation the right to claim the Africans and required the president of the United States to turn them over to Spain's representatives.

MURDER CHARGES DROPPED

At that point, the grand jury returned to the courtroom. The jurors asked for instructions on the murder charges before them. After a recess, the court made another momentous ruling. Circuit Court Judge Smith Thompson—who was also an associate justice on the U.S. Supreme Court—said the court had no jurisdiction in the alleged mutiny and murders since they occurred in international waters and did not involve U.S. citizens. Since it no longer had a case to consider, the grand jury was dismissed.

In addition to the duties of the high court, each Supreme Court justice was assigned to a specific circuit court and rode from one town to another to dispense justice. The justices also served with district court judges to hear appeals.

The only matters remaining to be decided were the claims of the Spaniards and the president's demand that the Africans be turned over to Spain—both of which claims would be heard in district court. Though an opponent of slavery, Judge Thompson ruled that the Africans, including the young girls, would have to remain in custody until the district court could sort out the competing claims in the case—and whether they were the property of the Spaniards. "However abhorrent it may be to our feelings, however desirable that every human being should be set at liberty, we cannot be governed by our feelings, but only by the law," he declared.

He scheduled a new hearing on the case for the third Tuesday in November. Tappan made arrangements for the young girls to live with the New Haven jailer, Colonel Stanton Pendleton, and his wife. In return, the girls acted as servants, doing housework and other chores.

An account in the *New York Herald*, well known for its antiabolitionist stance, reported that the abolitionists were "half frantic" that the judge had ordered that the Africans continue to be held in jail. "It would do your heart good to see the abolitionists since the decision of Judge Thompson. Poor devils!" the newspaper trumpeted. "They are chagrined beyond measure."

In truth, while disappointed that the Africans had not been freed, the *Amistad* team had won two points in circuit court: the murder and piracy charges against their clients had been dropped and the salvage claims had been dismissed. They now began to prepare for the upcoming hearing in district court.

A Native Speaker

Throughout the September trial, the *Amistad* lawyers had been hampered by not being able to communicate well with their clients. John Ferry had done his best, but he had difficulty understanding the prisoners' dialect and had not performed well in court. The defense team set out to find an interpreter who understood the Africans' language well enough to allow them to tell their story in court. They recruited Yale professor Josiah Gibbs, a noted linguist, to help them in their search. Using pantomime, the professor learned to count in the Africans' native tongue. Gibbs walked along the docks in New York to track down people who understood the African words. He wandered among the international crews, shouting "one," "two," "three," and so on in the mysterious dialect to anyone who might be of African descent.

A British sailor named James Covey recognized the words of his native language. Covey was from western Africa and, like most of the *Amistad* prisoners, was a member of the Mendi tribe. He, too, had been captured by slave traders when he was a child and taken to Lomboko, where he was sold into slavery. Now twenty, Covey had been rescued by a British navy crew on patrol for slave ships. After being freed, he had joined the navy to help in Britain's antislave trade efforts. The ship on which he served, the *Buzzard*, had docked in New York to buy needed supplies.

Gibbs also found another sailor, Charles Pratt, who could speak some Mendi. With the consent of their commanding officer, the two men agreed to interpret for the Africans in New Haven, with Covey as the main interpreter.

The Africans were ecstatic to finally be able to talk with

someone in Mendi. An account in the *New York Commercial Advertiser* reported that the interpreters arrived at the jail just as the prisoners were finishing breakfast. "One of the captives, coming to the door and finding one who could talk in his own language, took hold of him and literally dragged him in. Such a scene ensued as you may better conceive than I describe. Breakfast was forgotten; all crowded around the two men, and all talking as fast as possible. The children hugged one another with transport."

With Covey on the scene, the defense team now uncovered the rest of the Africans' story. Cinque himself would tell the captives' story in court, with Covey interpreting.

Spaniards in Jail

While waiting for the trial to begin in Hartford's district court, Tappan found a new way to stir things up and keep the public's interest in the case. In mid-October he filed suit on behalf of Cinque and another prisoner called Fulah, against the two Spaniards, Ruiz and Montes, for assault and false imprisonment. The suit sought two thousand dollars from each man as penalty for their acts. Tappan chose to issue the complaints in New York, where slavery was illegal. New York officials arrested the two men and placed them in jail.

Predictably, the action released a firestorm of outrage from the proslavery press and antiabolitionists. The *New York Herald* article describing the men's arrest at their hotel treated the Spaniards with great sympathy and Tappan with even greater disdain. The article portrayed Ruiz as an innocent victim without money for bail; Montes was reported to be "almost too sick and weak to get out of bed." Tappan, on the other hand, was accused of "ever deeper and intense malignity" and was compared to Judas Iscariot.

The Spanish minister to the United States, outraged at Tappan's suit, fired a protest off to Secretary of State John Forsyth demanding the Spaniards' release.

During the trial before the New York Court of Common Pleas, the Spaniards testified that they had paid for the slaves in good faith and had treated them well. Theodore Sedgwick, hired by Tappan, represented the Africans. He presented several affidavits to show that his clients had been taken from Africa and had not been slaves legally purchased in Cuba, as the Spaniards claimed. The terms of the treaty between the United States and Spain, the lawyer noted, banned the African slave trade.

On October 31, the judge in the New York case, after determining that Montes had not participated in any assault, released the older Spaniard without bail. The judge ordered Ruiz held on $250 bail. Montes fled to Cuba, but Ruiz chose to stay in jail for four months to win the public's sympathy for his position in the *Amistad* case.

An Expert Testifies

On November 19, 1839, Judge Andrew T. Judson convened the *Amistad* trial in the district court in Hartford. The Africans' lawyers tried to move the trial to New York, where the ship had first landed. Judson overruled their arguments and kept the trial in his jurisdiction.

Attorney Baldwin submitted his clients' plea to the court, that they "be hence dismissed and suffered to be and remain as they of right ought to be free & at liberty from the process of this Honorable court." In his plea, Baldwin argued that the captives had been born free in Africa and that the court had no right to hold them. When they took over the *Amistad*, Baldwin continued, his clients had acted as any free people might to win back their freedom—"Incited by the love of liberty natural to all men, and by the desire of returning to their families and kindred." When they landed in New York, "a place where Slavery did not exist," Baldwin noted, they had a right to expect the government to protect their freedom.

Lawyers for both the Spanish and U.S. governments also argued that the Africans be released—not to ensure their freedom, but to turn them over to Spain.

Covey, the Africans' interpreter, had fallen ill and had not been able to attend the proceedings. Because his services as interpreter were vital to the defense, the judge postponed the hearing until January 7, 1840. The new trial would be held in New Haven.

Before closing the session, the judge allowed a defense witness, Dr. Richard Robert Madden, to testify on the Cuban slave trade and other matters related to the case. Madden worked for the British in Cuba, overseeing Africans that had been freed there. After examining the *Amistad* prisoners, Madden told the court that he was sure they had recently come from Africa. He based his opinion on the Africans' looks, language, and manners. During his examination of the prisoners, Madden said, one of the captives had repeated a Muslim prayer Madden had recited to them in Arabic, a language common in Africa. He said that Africans learned Spanish quickly and abandoned their native languages after they had been in Cuba for a short time. He noted that the *Amistad* prisoners did not speak Spanish.

The British expert reiterated the terms of the international treaties that banned the importation of Africans to be sold as slaves in Cuba. He noted that Ruiz and Montes had obtained permits to buy Cuban-born slaves—known as "ladinos"—designed to disguise the Africans' origins. Such fraudulent documents could easily be obtained by paying a fee, Madden said. Slave traders, he added, were notorious for subverting the law in that way.

Cuban officials, he charged, "connive . . . and collude with the slave-traders." Even the governor was involved, receiving a bounty of ten dollars a head for each African brought into Havana.

Madden said he had visited the slave market where the *Amistad* captives had been sold and which was known for trading in slaves imported from Africa. An agent who had seen the *Amistad* captives there had told Madden he thought it was a pity that so many valuable Bozals would be lost if the blacks were freed. "Bozals" was the term given to slaves recently brought over from Africa.

Madden estimated that despite the international ban, traders had brought twenty thousand to twenty-five thousand illegal African slaves to Cuba in the past three years. "Such is the state of society, and of the administration of the laws there, that hopeless slavery is the inevitable result" for the Africans sold in Cuba and taken to America and other sites, Madden told the court.

The British expert's powerful testimony bolstered the defense argument that the *Amistad* prisoners had been illegally imported from Africa. It reflected Baldwin's contention that the court had the right to examine Ruiz's papers and determine whether they were fraudulent. Pinckney's Treaty, the lawyer argued, "could never have meant" that disputed rights rested solely on the word of officials. Such disputes, Baldwin said, had to be decided by "the same tribunals which, in all other cases, guard and maintain our civil rights."

"OLD MAN ELOQUENT"

The newspapers carried much discussion of the case as the public waited for the trial. John Quincy Adams, in a letter written November 19 and printed in the abolitionist newspaper *New York Journal of Commerce* on Christmas day, joined the fray on the side of the Africans. Adams

FORMER PRESIDENT JOHN QUINCY ADAMS ARGUED BEFORE THE U.S.
SUPREME COURT FOR THE RELEASE OF THE *AMISTAD* CAPTIVES.

certainly had the credentials as an American statesman to
comment on the issue. After serving as the sixth president
of the United States, Adams had won election as
Massachusetts representative in the U.S. Congress. The
son of one of the nation's founding fathers, he had earned
the nickname "Old Man Eloquent" for his speeches
against slavery on the House floor.

In his letter, Adams noted that the *Amistad* prisoners "were cast upon our coast in a condition perhaps as calamitous as could befall human beings." They were "victims of the African Slave Trade," Adams wrote, who "had vindicated their natural right to liberty, by conspiracy, insurrection, homicide and the capture of the ship in which they were embarked." The Africans deserved compassion, sympathy, and justice from "the humanity of a civilized nation." Instead, he noted, they were seized and brought to court on charges of murder and piracy. "Is this compassion?" Adams asked the readers. "Is it *sympathy*? Is it *justice*?"

In a follow-up letter printed in the same newspaper, Adams offered his services to the Africans' lawyers if "any service of mine would save the lives of those most distressed and most injured fellowmen." It was a pledge he would later be asked to keep.

four
Two Courts, One Result

On January 7, 1840, the attorneys, witnesses, the African prisoners, and curious onlookers gathered at New Haven's courthouse for the *Amistad* trial. Judge Judson once again presided. President Martin Van Buren fully expected his appointee to rule in favor of the Spaniards. So certain was Van Buren of the trial's outcome that he secretly ordered the USS *Grampus* to anchor in New Haven harbor. Once the judge had issued the expected ruling, U.S. Marshal Norris Willcox had been ordered to take the captives aboard the vessel before their lawyers could appeal the verdict. The *Grampus*, diverted from its usual duties as an antislavery patrol boat along the African coast, would then sail the captives to Cuba, where they would go on trial for piracy and murder. In addition, the president ordered lieutenants Gedney and Meade, officers on the *Washington* when the *Amistad* was first apprehended, to sail with the captives and testify at the Cuban trial.

The newspapers covering the trial carried no word of the *Grampus*'s secret mission. But some historians think Tappan, guessing Van Buren's intentions, planned to take the captives to Canada on a boat of his own if the verdict turned against them.

A raucous crowd waited impatiently for the trial to begin. In a letter to the *New York Journal of Commerce*, the

During the most dramatic moments of the *Amistad* trial, Cinque testifies about his capture in Africa, the miserable ocean crossing, and the captives' takeover of the *Amistad*.

Rev. H. G. Ludlow described the community's "thrilling interest" in the trial. "I can truly say that during no period of my life, save that in which my soul was deciding the question of its destiny for eternity, have my feelings been more intensely engaged," wrote Ludlow, a noted abolitionist. The community as a whole, he claimed, was inspired by the eloquence of the defense lawyers and "hung upon their lips spell bound." The other side, Ludlow grudgingly acknowledged, "was conducted as well perhaps as its badness permitted."

Testimony during the first day centered on the defense claims that the prisoners had been kidnapped from Africa. Several abolitionists gave evidence on the matter. The packed courtroom cheered enthusiastically after the *Amistad* prisoners' lawyer Roger Baldwin gave a stirring defense of liberty. Ludlow described the lawyer's performance as "irresistible," with "thoughts that breathed and words that burned." A stern Judge Judson rapped his gavel for quiet.

Dramatic Testimony

The trial's most dramatic moments occurred on the second day when Cinque and two other Africans testified. Even before the captives' statements, however, Judge Judson announced that he was convinced that they had been taken from Africa recently. He told the defense that they did not have to use the court's time to prove that fact.

Nevertheless, the defense proceeded with its plan to call on the Africans. Baldwin said his clients would testify on the jurisdictional question and would state that U.S. officers had seized them in New York, not Connecticut.

All eyes turned to the front of the courtroom as Cinque, wearing a blanket and accompanied by James Covey, solemnly made his way to the witness box. Every seat was filled.

In response to questions from Baldwin, Cinque began with a description of the shore party's meeting with Green. He soon shifted to the story of his kidnapping in Africa. Courtroom spectators listened to every word with "breathless attention," according to a newspaper account of the testimony.

Four Africans armed with a gun and knives had kidnapped him as he worked on a road near his home, Cinque told the court. The men took Cinque to Lomboko, the slave fortress in western Africa, along with four hundred men and two hundred women. There he met the men who would eventually sail with him aboard the *Amistad*. He first encountered the *Amistad* children in Havana.

Cinque told the court of his wife and his own three children back in Africa. At one point, Cinque sat on the courtroom floor to demonstrate the cramped quarters aboard the Portuguese slave ship, *Tecora*, that brought him to Havana. The captives had to lie side by side, chained together at their hands and feet, he said.

When they finally landed in Havana, they were kept in a prison with other slaves for ten days. Cinque described how Ruiz, accompanied by the man who had brought them from Africa, touched their bodies to see if they were healthy. Ruiz pointed out the captives he wanted to buy and took them to the ship *Amistad* for the journey to Port Principe.

Cinque's description of conditions aboard the Spanish ship was grim. During the trip from Havana, the captives were chained and beaten. Ruiz ordered four men to be whipped for stealing water, according to Cinque. The crew fed the captives half rations, only one plantain and two potatoes each per day. Cinque said the ship's cook signaled with his hands that their captors planned on eating the Africans. That led to the Africans' decision to take over the ship and attempt to return to their homeland.

Grabbaung and Fuliwa, two other African captives, confirmed Cinque's account. They said the captain had killed one of the Africans before being killed himself. Cinque, they said, killed the cook with a stick.

In other testimony, professor Josiah Gibbs and Covey disputed a report that Cinque had said he owned slaves in Africa or that he had been seized to repay a debt. After the testimony, the court adjourned for the day.

U.S. government lawyers called the captain's slave, Antonio, to the stand to testify the next day. They hoped that his version of events would make the court more sympathetic to the Spaniards. According to Antonio, the captives had plenty of food. But, he added, when the uprising began, the captain told him to throw bread at the Africans to calm them down. He said that Cinque had killed the captain with a cane knife two days after the ship left

Havana. The boy confirmed that the cook had told the Africans that the Spaniards intended to kill and eat them. He said he had no idea why the cook had said such a thing. The *Amistad*, he testified, carried slaves from Havana every two months. He also said that Ruiz had used the ship before to transport slaves.

After the dramatic testimony of the Africans and Antonio, onlookers had to sit through three days of tedious discussion of admiralty law and property claims.

A Surprising Ruling

Finally, on January 13, Judge Judson announced his decision. Out in the harbor, the USS *Grampus* stood ready to spirit away the Africans to Cuba. The courtroom, filled to overflowing, stilled as the judge, described as "gaunt and tense," read his ruling.

Judson first dealt with the salvage claims. Lieutenant Gedney, the judge ruled, had rendered a valuable service in rescuing the ship and preserving its cargo. For his efforts, Judson awarded the officer one third of the value of the ship and its cargo. The ship itself, the judge ruled, should be returned to the Spanish government.

The judge then turned to the question of the Africans. His decision surprised those on both sides of the issue. The Africans, Judson ruled, were free men, not the property of the Spaniards or anyone else. Spain itself had laws that banned the enslavement of Africans imported to Spanish lands after 1820. "If, by their own laws, they cannot enslave them, then it follows, of necessity, they cannot be demanded," the judge said. Judson ordered that the Africans be turned over to the president to be transported home to Africa, under the terms of the Act of 1819.

"Cinquez and Grabeau shall not sigh for Africa in vain," the judge decreed. "Bloody as may be their hands, they shall yet embrace their kindred."

Antonio was ordered to be returned to Havana, since he had been the captain's legal slave.

The verdict delighted abolitionists. Reverend Ludlow praised the judge for "showing an enlightened head and a warm heart." By deciding in favor of the Africans, the judge "immortalized his name," Ludlow wrote. The minister said that when he told Cinque and the rest of the Africans of the ruling, "they rose and fell down at my feet." One of the captives clapped his hands "for gladness of heart." The Africans longed to return home, Ludlow said. "Words cannot express the joy they felt." They knelt as he led them in a prayer of Thanksgiving.

The *Grampus*, its orders stymied by the judge's ruling, sailed out of New Haven harbor. The *New York Journal of Commerce*'s January 17 report on the vessel's movements was wrong on two counts. It surmised that the vessel had been sent to New Haven to transport the Africans home if the judge ordered. The ship left the harbor, the report said, because the Africans could not be removed before the appeal period ended. The newspaper predicted—also wrongly—that there would be no appeal.

U.S. Attorney William Holabird admitted that Judson's verdict "surprised everybody and no one more than myself." Acting on orders from Secretary of State Forsyth, he immediately appealed the judge's ruling to the circuit court. The only part of the decision the U.S. government did not appeal concerned the disposition of the slave Antonio.

After finally posting bail, Ruiz got out of jail in February, a month after Judson ruled against his claim on the Africans. The *New York Morning Herald* reported his release and urged that he be allowed to return to Cuba "free from further vexations and anxiety."

ANOTHER RULING, ANOTHER APPEAL

At the circuit court hearing in Hartford on April 29, Roger Baldwin and Seth Staples, once again representing the Africans, argued that the U.S. government had no right to file an appeal on behalf of foreign citizens. They asked Judge Smith Thompson, presiding over the hearing, to dismiss the government's appeal.

Thompson asked the lawyers to keep their arguments brief. He knew he would hear the debate again, when the decision was appealed to the high court, as he had no doubt it would be.

In early May 1840, Judge Thompson upheld the lower court's ruling to free the *Amistad* captives. Again, Holabird appealed the verdict "in pursuance of a demand made upon them by the duly Accredited Minister of Her Catholic Majesty the Queen of Spain." No one else, however, filed an appeal. The salvagers, the Spaniards, and the Spanish government left it in the hands of the U.S. government to pursue the case. The U.S. Supreme Court agreed to hear the case when it opened its next session in January 1841.

Tappan believed the Africans' case would be stronger if John Quincy Adams argued their cause before the Court. In October he convinced the aging former president to take on the case. Adams had won fame for his eloquent presentations before the Court, but the seventy-three-year-old Adams had not argued a case for more than thirty years. After agreeing to Tappan's request, Adams wrote in his diary, "I implore the mercy of God to control my temper, to enlighten my soul, and to give me utterance, that I may prove myself in every respect equal to the task." Adams spent the next several months studying every document and law related to the case.

FIVE
BEFORE THE SUPREME COURT

THE SUPREME COURT is the highest court in the land. As arbiter of the Constitution, it rules on questions of extreme importance to the entire nation. Neither the president nor Congress has the power to override its decisions. A Supreme Court decision on constitutional questions can be overturned only by another decision issued by a later Court or by a constitutional amendment. Only six U.S. Supreme Court decisions have been overruled by amendments to the Constitution. To overturn a Supreme Court decision that involves a law, Congress must pass a new law that meets constitutional requirements.

Usually the Court bases its decisions on precedent, rulings that previous Courts have made. Only in extreme circumstances does the Court reverse an earlier decision. By 1841 when the justices heard the *Amistad* case, the Supreme Court had reviewed few cases directly concerning slavery. The lower courts and the Supreme Court, however, had addressed the disposition of slaves aboard ships captured or disabled at sea. In 1822 Justice Joseph Story ruled on such a case in his role as circuit court judge. The case concerned the French schooner, *La Jeune Eugenie*, seized off the African coast by an American warship. The French vessel appeared to have been used in the slave trade, which the United States had banned in 1807.

ASSOCIATE JUSTICE JOSEPH STORY OPPOSED SLAVERY AND HAD RULED
AGAINST THE SLAVE TRADE IN A CIRCUIT COURT DECISION.

JUSTICES SPEAK THEIR MINDS: HOW SEPARATE OPINIONS INFLUENCE LAW

The U.S. Supreme Court is the highest court in the land. Its decisions are final. A Supreme Court decision can be overturned only by another decision issued by a later Court or by a constitutional amendment. Among the most notable decisions later invalidated was the *Dred Scott* ruling, in which the Court determined that blacks were not citizens and were not entitled to protection by the federal government. The decision was overturned by the Thirteenth and Fourteenth Amendments, which abolished slavery and established that everyone born in the United States was automatically a citizen with equal rights.

Usually the Court bases its decisions on precedent, rulings that previous Courts have made. Only in extreme circumstances does the Court reverse an earlier decision.

A ruling requires only a simple majority—five of the nine justices on a full Court. The majority opinion then establishes the law in the matter. The justices, appointed for life, each have an equal vote. Usually the chief justice, if he agrees with the majority, either writes the majority decision himself or appoints an associate justice also on the winning side to take on the task. When the chief justice is on the losing side, the most-senior associate justice who has voted with the majority makes the assignment.

Justices can write their own opinions on any case they wish. If they agree with the majority vote but have different reasons for their views, or want to comment on the case further, they can submit a concurrence. Those who disagree with a majority opinion can submit a dissent. Sometimes a justice writes a separate opinion so well that other justices are persuaded to join the dissent or concurrence.

Occasionally enough justices decide to join a separate opinion that it then becomes the majority opinion. Sometimes justices shift their support to a dissent, which then becomes the majority opinion.

Justice Tom Clark once said, "You know, we don't have money at the Court for an army, and we can't take ads in the newspapers, and we don't want to go out on a picket line in our robes. We have to convince the nation by the force of our opinions." That force can be—and occasionally is—undermined by opposing justices' separate opinions in a case. If a case is particularly controversial, a justice's separate opinion—sometimes concurring, but more often dissenting—can encourage continued opposition to the ruling. That is the reason Chief Justice Earl Warren worked so hard to get a unanimous ruling in the school desegregation case. And that is one reason why opponents to abortion continue to push for a ban on the procedure. In *Roe* v. *Wade*, the 1973 case that established the right of a woman to choose abortion, seven of the justices joined the majority position. However, in subsequent rulings, the vote has been much closer—often 5 to 4—in upholding the abortion right.

Because the Court relies so heavily on precedent, separate opinions play a key role when lawyers attempt to change the law. In *Brown* v. *Board of Education*, the lawyers arguing for school desegregation quoted Justice John Marshall Harlan's stinging dissent in *Plessy* v. *Ferguson*, the 1896 case that cemented segregation in place for more than half a century. Harlan had proclaimed the constitution "color-blind," and insisted that "the arbitrary separation of citizens on the basis of race . . . cannot be justified upon any legal grounds." Even though his views did not influence the Court at the time to reverse its stand, Harlan's prestige and eloquence helped persuade a more liberal Court years later.

In some cases, concurring justices' statements can explain and even strengthen the position taken in the majority opinion. A concurring opinion can also sometimes establish guidelines for future courts. For example, in the Pentagon Papers case (*New York Times* v. *United States*), the Court by a 6 to 3 vote allowed the *Times* and the *Washington Post* to print the Pentagon Papers, a massive, classified report on U.S. involvement in Vietnam. The written decision in this monumental case consisted of a single page and was issued per curiam. Per curiam means "by the court." Such a decision is unsigned, short, and usually on noncontroversial subjects. In the case of the Pentagon Papers, the Court may have issued a per curiam opinion because there was little time to develop a more in-depth opinion that would meet the approval of all six justices supporting the decision.

In allowing publication of the report, the Court's ruling stated only that the government had failed to meet "the heavy burden of showing justification for the enforcement of such a [prior] restraint [on a free press]."

Two concurring opinions went much further in bolstering freedom of the press and setting a precedent that future courts would use. Justices Byron White and Potter Stewart accepted the government's claim that publication of the report could damage the nation's war efforts. Even so, the justices refused to allow the government to stop the presses. The First Amendment, they stated in their concurring opinions, protected freedom of the press even in this case. Justice White wrote that the government could override the First Amendment's protection of the press only when publication resulted "in direct, immediate, and irreparable harm to our Nation, or its people." White's words became the standard on which future courts relied when determining cases involving national security and the press.

IN AN 1825 CASE, CHIEF JUSTICE JOHN MARSHALL RULED THAT SLAVES ABOARD A SHIP HAD TO BE RETURNED TO THEIR EUROPEAN OWNERS BECAUSE U.S. COURTS COULD NOT OVERRIDE THE LAWS OF OTHER NATIONS THAT ALLOWED THE SLAVE TRADE.

In his lower court ruling, Story attacked slavery and contended that the slave trade violated international law. Slave trading, he said, "is vindicated by no nation, and is admitted by almost all commercial nations as incurably unjust and inhuman."

The case never reached the Supreme Court. A similar case, involving a Spanish vessel, came before the high court in 1825. Chief Justice Marshall took an opposite stand in his majority opinion on the case. It revolved around the *Antelope*, a slave ship owned by Spanish and Portuguese traders. A group of Americans had captured the vessel and used it in the slave trade. Subsequently, U.S. warships had seized the ship, with almost three hundred slaves aboard, off the coast of Africa. The original owners from Spain and Portugal claimed ownership of the *Antelope* and its cargo of slaves.

In ruling for the foreign owners, Marshall said that one nation could not make laws for another. As long as Spain and Portugal allowed the slave trade, citizens of those countries had a right to conduct such business, even if other nations considered the activity immoral. Marshall ruled, however, that the foreign owners were entitled only to the slaves they had bought (and had documents for) before the Americans stole the ship.

MEMBERS OF THE COURT

For the first years of its existence, the U.S. Supreme Court operated with one chief justice and five associate justices, all appointed for life terms. To cope with a growing population, Congress added another justice to the Court in 1807. Two more justices were added to make nine in 1837, four years before the *Amistad* decision. Court membership jumped to ten in 1863, but three years after that Congress voted not to fill the next three seats that became vacant as justices died or retired.

In 1866 Congress passed the Judicial Circuits Act, which ratified the Court reduction plan, to prevent President Andrew Johnson from naming any appointees to the Court. Membership dipped to eight in 1867. Then, in 1869, Congress approved the Circuit Judges Act, which

set Court membership at nine. Since that time, nine justices serve on a full Court.

The expanded Court did not bode well for the *Amistad*
supporters. Lewis Tappan, the abolition leader who had
spearheaded the Africans' court battle, wrote that he had
"strong apprehensions" about the upcoming Court
hearing. The Court lineup certainly did not favor the
Africans and their abolitionist supporters. Of the nine
justices hearing the case, five were from the South
(including the two newest appointees), and several had
owned slaves, including the chief justice. A Maryland
native, Chief Justice Roger B. Taney came from a prominent family of slave-owning tobacco farmers. When
President Andrew Jackson appointed Taney to his post in
1835, a New York newspaper sniped, "The pure ermine of
the Supreme Court is sullied by the appointment of that
political hack, Roger B. Taney." The chief justice firmly
supported slavery and the Southern states' right to own
slaves. He would later rule with the majority in the *Dred
Scott* case that black men could not be U.S. citizens. But
the Court under his direction also protected the powers
of the federal government.

Associate Justice Joseph Story, appointed by President
James Madison in 1811 at the age of thirty-two, had served
longer than any other justice on the Court. A staunch
opponent of slavery, he had blasted the evils of the slave
trade in his 1822 circuit court decision involving the vessel
La Jeune Eugenie, an alleged slave runner. Even so, the
Massachusetts native held the Constitution in high esteem
and believed that slavery could be abolished gradually only
through changing the nation's laws.

Associate Justice Smith Thompson, who had already
ruled on the *Amistad* case in the circuit court, also
opposed slavery. He had been appointed to the Court by
President James Monroe in 1823. A New Yorker,

CHIEF JUSTICE ROGER B. TANEY WAS A MARYLAND NATIVE WHOSE FAMILY OWNED SLAVES. HE OVERSAW THE *AMISTAD* CASE WHEN IT CAME BEFORE THE SUPREME COURT IN 1841.

Thompson had been involved in state politics before serving on the Court and was active in many organizations, including the American Bible Society.

Associate Justice Henry Baldwin, a New Englander born in New Haven, Connecticut, took a middle stance between the states' rights position of Southerners and support for a strong federal government held by Story and others. Appointed to the Court in 1830 by Jackson, Baldwin had a reputation as a difficult personality who did not get along with the other justices.

Another Jackson appointee, Associate Justice John McLean, was born in New Jersey and moved to Ohio, where he attended law school. A vigorous antislavery advocate, he later became known as one of two justices to dissent in the *Dred Scott* case.

James M. Wayne, associate justice from Georgia, grew up on his family's rice plantation run by slave labor. Appointed by Jackson in 1835, he supported slavery but defended the Union.

Associate Justice Philip P. Barbour was one of the more ardent supporters of slavery on the Court. His slaveholding family owned extensive lands in Virginia. A Jackson appointee, he defended states' rights.

On his last day in office, President Jackson nominated John Catron to the Supreme Court as one of two new justices on the expanded Court. A businessman and lawyer from Tennessee, Catron had managed the presidential campaign of Martin Van Buren in his home state. He supported states' rights but did not believe in secession.

Associate Justice John McKinley, a Virginia native who spent most of his childhood in Kentucky, was another son of the South. Appointed by Van Buren to fill one of the two new seats on the Court, McKinley had little influence on the other members and rarely wrote opinions for the Court.

WAITING TO BE HEARD

The *Amistad* lawyers tried to get the Court to dismiss the case without a hearing. They argued that the government had no authority to plead the case at Spain's request. For a case to be heard at the Supreme Court level at that time, the value of property under dispute had to be worth at least two thousand dollars. Roger Baldwin and John Quincy Adams argued that if the *Amistad* Africans were considered slaves, they would be worth less than the required amount. It was a strange argument for antislavery advocates to make. Neither argument won a dismissal, and both sides continued with their preparations. Adams visited the Africans in Connecticut shortly after agreeing to take the case.

While awaiting the Supreme Court hearing, the *Amistad* Africans had been living in Westville, a small village outside New Haven. They had more freedom than they had while in jail, but still were in custody of the marshal.

In the months leading up to the Supreme Court hearing, Congress wrestled with the fallout from the *Amistad* case. In the Senate, John C. Calhoun, a strong proslavery advocate and former vice president, introduced a resolution that ships on the high seas fell under the sole jurisdiction of their country of origin. The Senate approved it.

In the House, Adams charged that the Van Buren administration had falsified documents pertinent to the *Amistad* case. In December 1840, Congress formed a committee to investigate the charges. Less than a month later, the House adopted the committee's report without issuing any penalty against the administration.

The Court had scheduled the *Amistad* hearing for January 1841. However, Justice Story was ill, and oral arguments in the case were postponed. The Court delayed the *Amistad* hearing again when arguments in other cases took longer than expected. Before the case could be argued in Court, District Attorney Holabird asked the circuit court for permission to sell the *Amistad* and its cargo. The long months of sitting idle during the wrangling in the courts had taken a toll on the ship. On October 15, 1840, the *Amistad* sold for $245 at public auction in New London, Connecticut; its contents garnered $6,196.14. The proceeds would be held by the circuit court until the Supreme Court ruled on who owned the property.

GILPIN STATES HIS CASE

Finally, on February 22, 1841, lawyers and spectators gathered in the Capitol Building in Washington, D.C., for the *Amistad* hearing. Without a building of its own, the Court was forced to use whatever room was available in the Old North Wing of the Capitol. Later, Congress designated a basement room beneath the Senate chambers for the Court. In 1861, after the Senate relocated to new quarters, the Court moved upstairs to the old Senate chambers. In 1935, the Supreme Court at long last settled into its own home, an ornate, marble temple of a building, adorned with massive columns inside and out.

All rose as Chief Justice Roger B. Taney, followed by the eight associate justices, entered the room. Attorney General Henry D. Gilpin would begin the proceedings with his arguments for the United States. Roger Baldwin would come next with his defense of the *Amistad* prisoners. He would be followed by John Quincy Adams for the *Amistad* position. Gilpin would make some concluding remarks to end the hearing.

Today, the Court receives up to nine thousand petitions for hearings each year. Justices select fewer than one hundred cases, which are heard in the next Court session. Each side is allotted only thirty minutes to present its case in oral arguments. Justices often interrupt the statements

THrouGH THE court sysTem

First Stop: State Court
Almost all cases (about 95 percent) start in state courts. These courts go by various names, depending on the state in which they operate: circuit, district, municipal, county, or superior. The case is tried and decided by a judge, a panel of judges, or a jury.

The side that loses can then appeal to the next level.

First Stop: Federal Court
U.S. DISTRICT COURT—About 5 percent of cases begin their journey in federal court. Most of these cases concern federal laws, the U.S. Constitution, or disputes that involve two or more states. They are heard in one of the ninety-four U.S. district courts in the nation.
U.S. COURT OF INTERNATIONAL TRADE—Federal court cases involving international trade appear in the U.S. Court of International Trade.
U.S. CLAIMS COURT—The U.S. Claims Court hears federal cases that involve more than $10,000, Indian claims, and some disputes with government contractors.

The loser in federal court can appeal to the next level.

Appeals: State Cases
Forty states have appeals courts that hear cases that have come from the state courts. In states without an appeals court, the case goes directly to the state supreme court.

Appeals: Federal Cases
U.S. CIRCUIT COURT—Cases appealed from U.S. district courts go to U.S. circuit courts of appeals. There are twelve circuit courts that handle cases from throughout the

nation. Each district court and every state and territory are assigned to one of the twelve circuits. Appeals in a few state cases—those that deal with rights guaranteed by the U.S. Constitution—are also heard in this court.

U.S. COURT OF APPEALS—Cases appealed from the U.S. Court of International Trade and the U.S. Claims Court are heard by the U.S. Court of Appeals for the Federal Circuit. Among the cases heard in this court are those involving patents and minor claims against the federal government.

Further Appeals: State Supreme Court

Cases appealed from state appeals courts go to the highest courts in the state—usually called supreme court. In New York, the state's highest court is called the court of appeals. Most state cases do not go beyond this point.

Final Appeals: U.S. Supreme Court

The U.S. Supreme Court is the highest court in the country. Its decision on a case is the final word. The Court decides issues that can affect every person in the nation. It has decided cases on slavery, abortion, school segregation, and many other important issues.

The Court selects the cases it will hear—usually around one hundred each year. Four of the nine justices must vote to consider a case in order for it to be heard. Almost all cases have been appealed from the lower courts (either state or federal).

Most people seeking a decision from the Court submit a petition for certiorari. Certiorari means that the case will be moved from a lower court to a higher court for review. The Court receives about nine thousand of these requests annually. The petition outlines the case and gives reasons why the Court should review it.

In rare cases, for example *New York Times* v. *United States*, an issue must be decided immediately. When such a case is of national importance, the Court allows it to bypass the usual lower court system and hears the case directly.

To win a spot on the Court's docket, a case must fall within one of the following categories:

- Disputes between states and the federal government or between two or more states. The Court also reviews cases involving ambassadors, consuls, and foreign ministers.

- Appeals from state courts that have ruled on a federal question.

- Appeals from federal appeals courts (about two-thirds of all requests fall into this category).

to ask questions and make their own comments. Any lawyer who goes beyond the time limit may look up to see the justices adjourning to their conference room beyond the thick red drapes that hang behind the bench.

In the first half of the nineteenth century, however, the Court had far fewer requests for hearings. Justices might sit for hours listening to the lawyers' remarks without interruption. In the *Amistad* case, oral arguments would occupy nearly five days.

At a signal from Chief Justice Taney, Gilpin rose and began his remarks.

The attorney general cited several cases in which the Court had ruled that documents granted by a foreign country had to be accepted as proof of ownership. It was not up to the officials of another country to determine whether the papers were issued erroneously:

> We are to inquire only whether the power existed, and whether it was exercised, and how it was exercised; not whether it was rightly or wrongly exercised.

If other nations took it upon themselves to second-guess the correctness of another nation's documents, chaos would ensue, according to Gilpin. He argued:

> Without such a rule, there could be no peace or comity among nations; all harmony, all mutual respect, would be destroyed; the courts and tribunals of one country would become the judges of the local laws and property of others.

Gilpin then examined the documents produced by Ruiz and Montes:

Here is the authentic certificate or record of the highest officer known to the Spanish law, declaring, in terms, that these negroes are the property of the several Spanish subjects. We have it countersigned by another of the principal officers. We have it executed and delivered, as the express evidence of property, to these persons. It is exactly the same as that deemed sufficient for the vessel and for the cargo.

Based on that reasoning, Gilpin concluded that the ship and its cargo should be considered the property of the Spanish owners.

Then he raised the question central to the case: "Is there any difference between property in slaves and other property?" In answering the question, Gilpin noted that both Spain and the United States considered slaves to be property. Even in states where slavery had been abolished, laws required runaway slaves, if found, to be returned to their proper owners.

In addition, the Court did not have the authority to question the papers produced by Ruiz and Montes showing that they had bought the slaves any more than it could discount the documents on the ship and its cargo, Gilpin argued.

If the *Amistad* captives recently came from Africa, as appeared to be the case, what "special law or decree" could be cited to prove they should not be considered slaves, Gilpin asked the Court. The 1817 treaty between England and Spain, as well as several other documents, did not apply in the case, he said, because there was no proof that the *Amistad* captives had been free in Cuba. The captives "had not been 'declared free,' by any competent tribunal," he told the Court. "Even had they been taken actually on board of a vessel engaged in the slave trade, they must have been adjudicated upon at one of the two special courts, and nowhere else." Without a ruling from the Spanish courts that the captives had been imported illegally, Gilpin argued, the U.S. courts had no jurisdiction in the case.

Gilpin referred to the cases of the *Antelope* and *La Jeune Eugenie*, among others, in making his point that the United States had many times returned ships to officials from the countries where they originated. "It is thus settled," he told the Court, "that the public functionaries are entitled to intervene in such cases, on behalf of the citizens of their countries."

The slaves, he concluded, should be treated like the rest of the cargo aboard the *Amistad* and turned over to Spain, as representative of the owners.

SIX
FOR THE DEFENSE

DURING THE AFTERNOON SESSION, Roger Baldwin began his arguments in the *Amistad* case. He spoke for the thirty-six Africans of the *Amistad* still alive. Since their capture and imprisonment in New Haven in August 1839, thirteen of the prisoners had died of illness.

Baldwin began by paying tribute to the Court as a "tribunal . . . elevated far above the influence of Executive power and popular prejudice." He criticized the governments of the United States and Spain for trying "to disturb the course of justice" by inflaming citizens with attacks in the press against the judge and the Africans.

The *Amistad* case, Baldwin noted, went far beyond the Africans involved. "It involves considerations deeply affecting our national character in the eyes of the whole civilized world, as well as questions of power on the part of the government of the United States, which are regarded with anxiety and alarm by a large portion of our citizens."

In making his argument, Baldwin was keenly aware of the controversy over states' rights and tried not to offend those who passionately defended such rights. "I have ever been of the opinion that the exercise of that liberty by citizens of one State in regard to the institutions of another should always be guided by discretion, and tempered with kindness."

Attorney Roger Sherman Baldwin, a leading abolitionist, argued that the *Amistad* captives had been enslaved illegally and should be freed by the Court and allowed to return home to Africa.

A MATTER OF FREEDOM

The lawyer posed the question at the heart of his case: Did the United States government have the right to force slavery on free men "cast upon our shores"? In answering this question, he outlined for the Court the details of the case, tracing the movements of the Africans and relating the lower court proceedings.

Baldwin said that the Africans "were in the actual condition of freedom" when they arrived in New York. "They were in a state where, not only no law existed to make them slaves, but where, by an express statute, all persons, except fugitives . . . from a sister state, are declared to be free," the lawyer told the Court.

It was not the role of the U.S. government, he added, to enslave people at the request of foreign nations. Most Americans, he said, would find such government activities repugnant as well as a violation of the nation's fundamental principles.

If a foreign slave vessel, engaged in a traffic which by our laws is denounced as inhuman and piratical, should be captured by the slaves while on her voyage from Africa to Cuba, and they should succeed in reaching our shores, have the Constitution or laws of the United States imposed upon our judges, our naval officers, or our executive, the duty of seizing the unhappy fugitives and delivering them up to their oppressors? Did the people of the United States, whose government is based on the great principles of the Revolution, proclaimed in the Declaration of Independence, confer upon the federal, executive, or judicial tribunals, the power of making our nation accessories to such atrocious violations of human right?

Baldwin argued that his clients' case differed from that of the *Antelope*, the Spanish slave ship seized by Americans. Unlike the Africans aboard the *Antelope*, the *Amistad* blacks were not slaves when their ship was seized by U.S. officers. "They appear here freemen," Baldwin asserted. As free individuals, the Africans should be considered "on equal ground" with the Spaniards in the case, he said. New York law required that a foreign slave who escaped to that state would become free, Baldwin said. He cited French and English laws with similar requirements.

Baldwin acknowledged that international treaties regulating piracy stipulated that all recovered merchandise should be returned to the owners of the rescued vessel. But he denied that the term "merchandise" included slaves. The treaties contained "no special reference to human beings as property," he noted, and it could not be assumed that humans were considered merchandise, especially in states and nations that banned slavery.

Baldwin commented that it would be strange indeed if the Court ruled that the 1819 treaty required the United States to treat the slave trade's victims as property when that same treaty pledged nations "to promote [the slave trade's] entire abolition, as a traffic irreconcilable with the principles of humanity and justice."

Neither should his clients be viewed as pirates, Baldwin told the Court. In seizing the *Amistad*, Cinque— "the master-spirit who guided them," in Baldwin's words—aimed only to free himself and his companions. They took over the ship and killed the crew so that they could return to their homes. "In so doing," Baldwin said, "they were guilty of no crime, for which they could be held responsible as pirates." He noted that if American seamen had been captured and eventually killed their captors to free themselves, they would not be guilty of a crime. Baldwin quoted former Chief Justice John Marshall's words on the topic regarding another case:

> The act of impressing an American is an act of lawless violence. The confinement on board a vessel is a continuation of that violence, and an additional outrage. Death committed within the United States in resisting such violence, would not have been murder.

WHERE'S THE PROOF?

Addressing the claims of Ruiz and Montes, Baldwin argued that the two Spaniards had not proved that the Africans were slaves. Certainly they were not slaves under New York law, where slavery had been abolished. They might have been slaves under Cuban law, if they had lived there. Baldwin made a convincing argument that his clients had never been residents of Cuba. Their ten days in jail there did not mean that they had willingly given up their homes in Africa. "These victims of fraud and piracy—husbands torn from their wives and families—children from their parents and kindred—neither intended to abandon the land of their nativity, nor had lost all hope of recovering it," Baldwin told the justices. Even Cuba, which allowed slavery, did not have laws that transformed men born free in Africa into slaves, Baldwin noted.

"If they are slaves, then," the lawyer continued, "it must be by some positive law of Spain [which claimed jurisdiction over Cuba], existing at the time of their recent importation." But, he concluded, "there has been no such law in force there, either statute or common law." In fact, Baldwin said, Spain had adopted laws to *prevent* the enslavement of Africans brought to Cuba. Spain had not only signed a treaty banning the slave trade as of 1820 but had issued an ordinance in 1817 requiring "that every

African imported into any of the colonies of Spain in violation of the treaty, shall be declared free in the first port at which he shall arrive." A treaty between Spain and Great Britain in 1835 reiterated that Spain had "totally and finally abolished" the slave trade "in all parts of the world," Baldwin pointed out.

The lawyer turned his attention next to the attorney general's contention that the United States had no power to question the validity of documents issued by another nation. Ruiz and Montes, Baldwin told the Court, had committed fraud. Their papers referred to Cuban-born slaves, not free-born Africans. By uncovering the fraud and not allowing the traders to get away with it, the United States would be enforcing the laws of Spain. He noted that in the year and a half since district court had ruled against the two Spaniards, "not a particle of evidence has since been produced in support of their claims."

"And yet," Baldwin said, a touch of outrage evident as he concluded his remarks, "strange as it may seem, during all this time, not only the sympathies of the Spanish minister, but the powerful aid of our own government have been enlisted in their behalf!"

With that Baldwin sat down. He had spoken ardently on behalf of his clients for a day and a half. On the following day, February 24, the justices would turn their attention to the arguments of John Quincy Adams.

OLD MAN ELOQUENT SPEAKS HIS MIND

As a former president and current member of the House of Representatives, John Quincy Adams drew much attention as he made his way to the front of the courtroom. He had not argued a case for thirty years. The audience might well have wondered if the old man had the stamina for the job. They would soon learn the seventy-three-year-old Adams had energy to spare.

Although noted for his eloquence, Adams had made many enemies over the course of his long and combative political career. He would face six justices appointed by his old nemesis Andrew Jackson. In 1824 Jackson had won the popular vote for president, but the House of Representatives awarded the post to Adams when neither candidate won a majority of electoral college votes. Jackson defeated Adams in his bid for reelection four years later.

Adams began with an apology to the Court for his failings. "I shall perhaps be more likely to exhibit at once the infirmities of age and the inexperience of youth, than to render . . . services [to my clients]." But he quickly proceeded to the task at hand.

Asking that the justices treat each of the Africans as an individual, Adams called on the Court to consider "that the life and the liberty of every one of them must be determined by its decision for himself alone." He charged that the Van Buren administration had sided early on with Spanish slave traders against "these poor, unfortunate, helpless, tongueless, defenseless Africans."

The appeal should be dismissed and the Africans freed, Adams told the Court. He based his case on the argument that the United States should never have seized the *Amistad*, or the Africans, in the first place. "The proceedings on the part of the United States are all wrongful from the beginning," he said.

In making his case, he reiterated the demands of the Spanish minister and the appeasing responses of American officials. According to Adams, the United States should have immediately rejected Spain's claims and left it to the courts to decide the claims on property. The Africans, he argued, should be set free.

As evening approached, Chief Justice Taney adjourned Court for the day. Adams was scheduled to resume his argument in the morning.

Tragic news

The next day, on Wednesday, word reached the Court that Associate Justice Barbour had died unexpectedly during the night. The visibly shaken justices took their seats, and Chief Justice Taney, after announcing the sad news, adjourned the Court until the following Monday.

On March 1, after a brief Court ceremony honoring Barbour, Adams resumed his oration. Opening with condolences for the dead justice, he restated his confidence in the Court as a "Court of Justice." He said he planned to show the errors committed by the president and others in the case, but he assured the Court that he held "no unkind sentiments" toward any of his opponents. Adams said he had tried to convince the president not to pursue the case in court, but when that failed, Adams said he was forced to defend the Africans.

Despite his disclaimer to the contrary, Adams lobbed a virulent attack against President Van Buren. He gave a long, detailed description of the political intrigues swirling around the case. Much of the discussion focused on the president's secret instructions to the *Grampus*, posted in New Haven harbor with orders to take the captives back to Cuba. Adams told the Court he was astonished by the former attorney general's opinion, issued before the lower court hearings had concluded, that the Africans should be turned over to Spain. After reading the document to the Court, Adams exclaimed, "I am ashamed to stand up before the nations of the earth, with such an opinion recorded as official, and what is worse, as having been adopted by the government." Adams charged, as he had in Congress, that documents in the case had been falsified.

On another point, the feisty orator questioned the legitimacy of the documents Ruiz and Montes said proved they had bought the slaves in Cuba. The papers, Adams

LIFE as a supreme court justice in the 1800s

U.S. Supreme Court justices had a rigorous schedule in the first half of the 1800s when the *Amistad* case was tried. In addition to the duties required by the Supreme Court, each justice was assigned to at least one circuit court. This meant that the justice not only had to travel to Washington, D.C., to attend Supreme Court hearings and conferences during the winter months; he also had to travel from town to town presiding at circuit courts under his jurisdiction. Justices also sat with district court judges to hear appeals. Associate Justice Joseph Story, for example, traveled more than two thousand miles a year to dispense justice in the circuit courts of Maine, New Hampshire, Rhode Island, and Massachusetts. Before automobiles, interstate commuter trains, and air travel, justices rode on horseback or in horse-drawn carriages over often-dangerous roads.

Most of the justices stayed in boardinghouses along Pennsylvania Avenue when the Supreme Court was in session. Among the more noted was Elizabeth Peyton's house at the intersection of Pennsylvania Avenue and 4-1/2 Street. There Chief Justice John Marshall, Associate Justice Story, and Senators John C. Calhoun and Henry Clay, among others, spent their evenings discussing the issues of the day.

Chief Justice Marshall encouraged his fellow justices to live together at the same boardinghouse during Court sessions. Marshall believed that such living arrangements brought justices closer together and led to unanimous decisions. Such appeared to be the case; the Marshall Court handed down one unanimous ruling after another during the course of almost thirty-five years.

According to Justice Story, he and his colleagues spent many evenings discussing cases at the boardinghouse:

> [We] live in the most frank and unaffected intimacy . . . united as one, with a mutual esteem which makes even the labors of jurisprudence light . . . we [discuss] every question as we proceed, and familiar conferences at our lodgings often come to a very quick and, I trust, a very accurate opinion, in a few hours.

All was not work, however. Story noted, "Our social hours . . . are passed in gay and frank conversation."

During the *Amistad* case, the justices, as usual, stayed at a Pennsylvania Avenue boardinghouse. After a full day in Court listening to John Quincy Adams's address on February 24, 1841, the justices discussed the case until about 10 p.m. All reports said Justice Philip Barbour was in good spirits when he went to his room in the boardinghouse that night. On the following morning, a servant at the boardinghouse knocked on the justices' doors to call them to breakfast. When he heard no reply from Justice Barbour, he opened the door and discovered him dead in his bed. He summoned Chief Justice Roger B. Taney, who confirmed that his associate had died during the night, apparently in his sleep. "Not a muscle was distorted, nor were the bedclothes in the slightest degree disturbed," the *New York Journal of Commerce* reported. "It is probable his heart ceased to beat in an instant." Barbour was fifty-seven years old at the time of his death.

The Court recessed for a few days to honor him and allow the justices to attend the funeral. On March 1, John Quincy Adams resumed his arguments in the *Amistad* case.

contended, did not even describe each African. "How is this Court to ascertain, that the persons named in this paper are the same with those taken in the *Amistad*?" he asked. "No court, no tribunal, no officer, would accept such a document as a passport."

To reinforce his point, Adams reviewed the *Antelope* case at length. Like Baldwin, he noted that in the previous case—"this unblushing bargain and sale of human captives"—the Supreme Court had required the Spanish to provide proof of which slaves aboard the *Antelope* had been theirs. He noted, too, that Chief Justice John Marshall had declared that "no principle is settled" in the decision in the case. Therefore, Adams argued, the *Antelope*'s outcome—the return of the slaves—should not be used as a basis for the *Amistad* or any other case.

In calling for the Africans' release, Adams quoted the Declaration of Independence, which his father, John Adams, had signed. "The moment you come to the Declaration of Independence, that every man has a right to life and liberty, an inalienable right, this case is decided," he told the Court. "I ask nothing more in behalf of these unfortunate men, than this Declaration."

Dramatic Farewell

Adams closed his final appearance before the Supreme Court with a dramatic farewell. "Little did I imagine that I should ever again be required to claim the right of appearing in the capacity of an officer of this Court; yet such has been the dictate of my destiny—and I appear again to plead the cause of justice, and now of liberty and life, in behalf of many of my fellow men." Calling upon justices long dead, he intoned, "Where are they all? Gone! Gone! All gone!" He directed his final words to the current members of the Court: a prayer that "after the close of a long and virtuous career," they might "be received at the portals of the next with the approving sentence—'Well done, good and faithful servant; enter thou into the joy of thy Lord.'"

Adams's oration stretched over two days. Listeners might have been stirred by Adams's passionate words, but in the end the Court would rely much more heavily on Roger Baldwin's arguments. The Court reporter, frustrated in his attempts to get a copy of Adams's remarks for the record, noted later that the Court had not considered many of Adams's points "essential to its decision" and the former president's remarks "were not taken notice of in the opinion of the Court."

On March 2, Attorney General Gilpin followed Adams's lengthy oratory with a brief summation of his arguments in the case. The fate of Cinque and his compatriots now lay in the hands of the Court.

THE AFRICANS OF THE *AMISTAD* REJOICE AS THEY SET FOOT ON AFRICAN SOIL THREE YEARS AFTER BEING KIDNAPPED AND TAKEN TO CUBA.

seven
DECISION AND AFTERMATH

ON MARCH 9, 1841, Justice Joseph Story issued the U.S. Supreme Court's decision in the *Amistad* case. Upholding the lower courts' opinion, the Court ruled that the Africans were free men. While it did not attack slavery, the ruling acknowledged that the Africans had rights equal to those of the Spaniards making the claims against them. "The United States," Story noted, "are bound to respect their [the Africans'] rights as much as those of Spanish subjects."

Story ordered the immediate release of the Africans. The opinion also upheld the salvage claims of Thomas R. Gedney and ordered that he be paid one-third of the proceeds from the *Amistad* and its cargo. Story further ruled that the Act of 1819 did not apply to the case, since the Africans were not brought as slaves to the United States but arrived there as free people. That being the case, Story struck down the lower court's order that the U.S. government return the Africans to their homeland. Under the Supreme Court ruling, the Africans were free to go, but the U.S. government would have no further dealings with them.

All the Southerners on the Court supported the opinion. Only Justice Henry Baldwin of the eight remaining justices dissented, offering no comment on the case.

Noting that the case had been "very elaborately

argued"—a nod, no doubt, to John Quincy Adams's tour de force—Story distilled the arguments into three pleas:

> 1. The United States requested only that the Spanish claimants be given their property.
> 2. Lieutenant Gedney asked for his claim to salvage for his role in rescuing the *Amistad*.
> 3. The third party to the case, the Africans, claimed to be kidnapped and sought their freedom.

The major controversy arose, of course, over whether the Africans could legitimately be considered property. According to Story, they could not. The *Amistad* Africans had never been lawful slaves and therefore had to be considered free men, Story declared.

> They are natives of Africa, and were kidnapped there, and were unlawfully transported to Cuba, in violation of the laws and treaties of Spain, and the most solemn edicts and declarations of that government.

narrow Decision

The decision was a narrow one. Story avoided a broad ruling that could have been interpreted by the South as an attempt to abolish slavery on a national level. In fact, the opinion upheld the institution of slavery by ordering that the slave Antonio be returned to his owner's family. In addition, Story's opinion acknowledged that blacks could be considered property and would have been included in the merchandise returned to the owners if they had been "lawfully held as slaves, under the laws of Spain."

The decision did, however, strike a blow against the slave trade, which Story noted had been "utterly abolished" by international treaties. "The dealing in that trade," he stated, "is deemed a heinous crime."

The justice also discarded the notion that the Africans had been guilty of piracy and murder:

> We may lament the dreadful acts by which they asserted their liberty, and took possession of the *Amistad*, and endeavored to regain their native country; but they cannot be deemed pirates or robbers, in the sense of the law of nations, or the treaty with Spain, or the laws of Spain itself.

Story rejected the argument made by Attorney General Henry D. Gilpin that U.S. courts had no authority to question documents issued by another nation. When documents were proved to be fraudulent, Story said, "it overthrows all their sanctity, and destroys them as proof. Fraud will vitiate any, even the most solemn, transactions; and an asserted title to property, founded upon it, is utterly void." Illustrating his point, the justice noted that American officials would have every right to investigate a foreign ship entering a U.S. port suspected of disguising its country of origin. "There can be no doubt, that it would be the duty of our courts to strip off the disguise, and to look at the case, according to its naked realities."

Despite the ruling's failure to strike down slavery, the abolitionists hailed the decision as a victory. In a news-paper announcement of the decision a week later, the Amistad Committee proclaimed the "great deliverance" of the Africans and its "high satisfaction" with the opinion. "The Supreme Court of the United States have definitely decided that our long-imprisoned brethren who were taken in the schooner *Amistad*, ARE FREE on this soil, without condition or restraint," read the announcement. The opinion, according to the notice, also established "many fundamental principles of law, justice, and human rights."

After the Court issued its decision, the case returned to circuit court for a final settlement of claims. Justice Thompson presided over the hearing, held during the April term. According to court records, one-third of the proceeds went to Lieutenant Gedney, Jose Antonio Tellincas (owner of the vessel) was awarded $313.38, the firm of Aspa & Laca received $577.21 for merchandise lost, and $972.04 was set aside for any future claims. Jose Ruiz and Pedro Montes, who had to pay fees, taxes, and salvage costs, ultimately received nothing.

The *Amistad* case appeared before the courts one last time in April 1845 when a Cuban merchant filed suit in the U.S. Circuit Court in Connecticut in hopes of recovering the cost of merchandise he lost aboard the *Amistad*. The merchant, Ramon Bermejo, received $631 for his trouble.

NOT a traditional Landmark case

The *Amistad* opinion was not a landmark decision in the usual sense of the term. The Court's ruling did not change the course of U.S. history. Subsequent Court opinions did not cite the case in making new decisions. Although the case increased tensions between the North and South for a time, other events had a far greater impact on the national debate over slavery that ultimately led to the Civil War.

A similar slave rebellion eight months after the Supreme Court decision ended with a different outcome. The incident occurred aboard the U.S. vessel *Creole*, which was transporting slaves from Virginia to New Orleans. Unlike the *Amistad* blacks, the slaves had been legally purchased. Madison Washington, one of the slaves aboard, led a small group in a revolt that overpowered the crew of the *Creole* and commandeered the ship to the Bahamas, a British colony.

British authorities in the Bahamas ruled that local laws applied to the case. Since Britain had ended slavery in its colonies in 1833, the British officials freed the slaves. The South erupted in outrage. With some members of Congress threatening war, Secretary of State Daniel Webster demanded that Britain reimburse the slaveholders for their losses. In a compromise, the British agreed not to assist slaves who tried to escape in the future. They eventually paid $110,000 to the owners of the *Creole*, which was never returned.

The involvement of President Martin Van Buren in the case seemed to have little effect on the presidential campaign that year. Both Van Buren and his opponent William Henry Harrison spoke out against abolitionists and defended slavery. The *Emancipator* newspaper considered Harrison a bigger friend of slavery than Van Buren, despite the president's actions in the *Amistad* case. Van Buren lost, and Harrison died one month after taking office.

The *Amistad* case failed to alter slavery opinions on the high court. In 1857, sixteen years after the *Amistad* decision, the U.S. Supreme Court, with many of the same justices still sitting on the bench, held in the *Dred Scott* case that blacks had "no rights which the white man was bound to respect." Dred Scott, a slave who lived in the free states of Illinois and Minnesota, had sued for his freedom when he was returned to the slave state of Missouri. Chief Justice Roger B. Taney wrote in his majority opinion that the U.S. Constitution was never intended to include slaves in its protections. "It is too clear for dispute," Taney wrote, "that the enslaved African race were not intended to be included, and formed no part of the people who framed and adopted this declaration."

It would be the last attempt to settle the slavery issue in the courts. In December 1860, South Carolina seceded

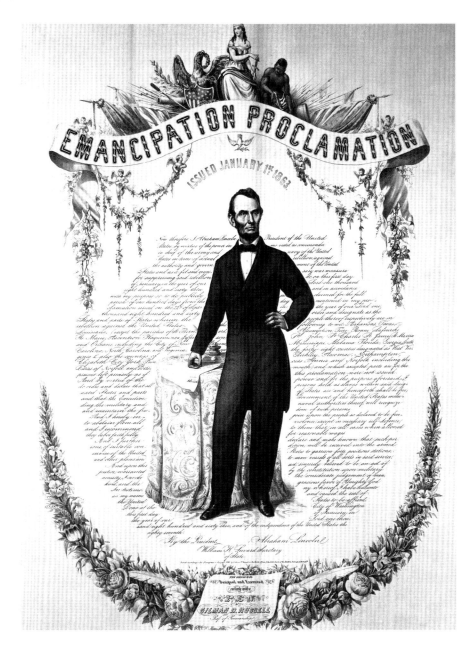

PRESIDENT ABRAHAM LINCOLN FREED ALL U.S. SLAVES AND ABOLISHED
SLAVERY WHEN HE ISSUED THE EMANCIPATION PROCLAMATION IN 1863.

from the Union, following the election of Abraham Lincoln to the presidency. Six other states seceded in the next two months, and the Confederate States of America was formed. With the firing of Confederate guns on Fort Sumter in Charleston, South Carolina, the Civil War began.

On January 1, 1863, President Lincoln issued the Emancipation Proclamation freeing the slaves and abolishing slavery: "I do order and declare that all persons held as slaves within said designated States, and parts of States, are, and henceforward shall be free."

The first section of the Fourteenth Amendment finally overturned the *Dred Scott* opinion. With the passage of the amendment, ratified in 1868, "all persons born or naturalized in the United States," including former slaves, became citizens of the United States, and of the state where they lived.

The slave trade continued for many years after the *Amistad* incident. British efforts to stop the trade gradually reduced the international traffic in slaves. In 1840 the British navy raided slave factories along the Gallinas River, but it was not until 1849 that the British navy destroyed the slave factory at Lomboko, where Cinque and the others had been held. The signing of the Webster-Ashburn Treaty of 1842—which settled the border of northern Maine and Canada—improved cooperation between the United States and Britain. The two nations worked together to suppress the slave trade. The demand for slaves that fueled the trade disappeared when Brazil became the last country to abolish slavery in 1888.

Spain deplored the *Amistad* verdict and for two decades pressed the United States for compensation. In defiance of the *Amistad* decision, presidents James Polk, Franklin Pierce, and James Buchanan all tried to convince Congress to pay Spain for the loss of the *Amistad* captives.

Congress refused to buckle to presidential pressure under the leadership of opponents like Congressman Joshua Giddings of Ohio, who railed against the "exceedingly dangerous" precedent of indemnifying Spain. Spain finally gave up when the American Civil War began.

Impact of the *Amistad* case

In other ways, however, the *Amistad* case did make a difference. To the Africans involved, of course, the decision restored their freedom and possibly saved their lives. Since the Supreme Court had overruled the lower court's order that the U.S. government transport the *Amistad* blacks back to Africa, it fell to the abolitionists to get them home. After the case ended, they moved the Africans to Farmington, Connecticut, where they were soon joined by the young girls who had been living with the jailer, Colonel Stanton Pendleton, and his wife. The abolitionists provided food and clothing, taught them English, and tried to convert them to Christianity. To raise money for the Africans' care and the eventual trip to Africa, the abolitionists took the blacks on tour. Several thousand people paid fifty cents apiece to see the Africans perform at New York City's Broadway Tabernacle on May 14, 1841. To rousing cheers from a racially mixed audience, the Africans recited spelling lessons, read from the Bible, sang hymns, and recounted their days of captivity.

The cabin boy Antonio disappeared after the Court ruled that he was a slave and should be returned to the captain's family. He was later sighted in Canada. Lewis Tappan and the abolitionists aided him in his escape.

In August, the African known as Foone died from drowning. Some speculated that he committed suicide because he could no longer bear to be away from home. His death spurred the abolitionists to speed up preparations for the trip to Africa.

FARMINGTON, CONNECTICUT, AS VIEWED FROM THE NORTHWEST. AFTER THE
SUPREME COURT DECISION THAT FREED THEM, THE *AMISTAD* MEN AND CHIL-
DREN LIVED IN THIS TOWN UNTIL MONEY COULD BE RAISED FOR THEIR RETURN
TO AFRICA.

The Amistad Committee raised more funds, and on November 27, the thirty-five surviving Africans boarded the *Gentleman* and sailed out of New York harbor headed for Sierra Leone. Lewis Tappan presented all with a farewell gift, led them in the Lord's Prayer, then stood watching as the bark sailed east toward Africa. He later wrote a friend, "The spirit of liberty, I am happy to say is rising."

The *Gentleman* sailed into Freetown, Sierra Leone, in pJanuary 1842. Cinque had not seen his homeland for three years. Mendi friends and neighbors excitedly greeted the returning Africans. But Cinque's family was not among the well-wishers. He soon discovered that his wife and children had been killed and his village destroyed in wars over the slave trade.

The Africans' journey home also marked the beginning of a new campaign by the *Amistad* abolitionists, that of saving souls in Africa. Five Americans, including two ministers, accompanied the Africans to their homeland. They headed an effort to establish a Christian mission among the Mendi people. Several of the *Amistad* Africans, including Cinque, lived and worked at the mission initially. Cinque, however, left the mission soon after arriving in Africa. His life after that is shrouded in speculation and unconfirmed rumors.

The Rev. James W. C. Pennington, a former slave and pastor of the First Colored Congregational Church in Hartford, founded the Union Missionary Society to spearhead the effort in Africa. It later merged to become the American Missionary Association (AMA). The AMA, the nation's foremost abolitionist society in the years leading up to the Civil War, also pursued ambitious educational and religious goals. It supported elementary and secondary schools for blacks, helped found seven colleges, and conducted other projects. The United Church of

Christ's missionary arm, United Church Board for Homeland Ministries, is today an outgrowth of the original AMA group that raised money for the Mendi mission in Africa.

The AMA merged with other antislavery groups in 1846 to expand the missions that served Africans as well as freed slaves from the United States. A strange mix of groups supported the effort to send freed slaves to Africa. Abolitionists wanted to provide former slaves with a better life and hoped to convert Africans to Christianity. They joined with slave owners whose goal was to get rid of free blacks, who they feared would stir up slaves and lead revolts against slavery. The return of the *Amistad* Africans and the establishment of a mission in their homeland helped focus more attention on the colonization effort. In 1847, one of the African missions established earlier by the American Colonization Society became the independent nation of Liberia.

The *Amistad* case also reinvigorated the abolitionist movement in the North. It helped unite the fragmented groups behind the Africans' cause. Years later, Tappan appeared at a gathering to celebrate President Abraham Lincoln's signing of the Emancipation Proclamation. As the crowd turned its attention to the old freedom fighter, he read the letter John Quincy Adams had sent telling him of the Supreme Court's decision in the *Amistad* case. Antislavery forces still savored the victory.

CINQUE AS HERO

"Cinque will continue to be an object of interest, and his name will be the watchword of freedom to Africa and her enslaved sons throughout the world," the author of a letter to the editor of the *Emancipator* had predicted soon after the decision. The prediction proved true—but Cinque's greatest fame would be realized in another century.

During the twentieth century, Cinque and the *Amistad* Africans became symbols of freedom for new generations of black Americans embroiled in their own struggle for civil rights.

Cinque inspired the leader of a dubious radical group in the 1970s. Donald DeFreeze, a black man who escaped from prison in California and formed the Symbionese Liberation Army (SLA), renamed himself Cinque Mtune after Cinque of the *Amistad*. While the original Cinque fought for his freedom, Cinque Mtune led a mostly white, middle-class group that used murder, kidnapping, and bank robbery to create headlines and make political statements. They won worldwide attention after kidnapping newspaper heiress Patty Hearst. Cinque Mtune and five other SLA members were later killed in a battle with police in an SLA safe house near Los Angeles.

In 1997 filmmaker Steven Spielberg captured Cinque's moment in history on screen with his release of the $70 million movie epic *Amistad*. The movie starred Morgan Freeman as a fictional black abolitionist, Anthony Hopkins as a curmudgeonly John Quincy Adams, and the unknown West African model Djimon Hounsou as the commanding Cinque. The movie contained many historical inaccuracies, including the misleading impression that the Supreme Court decision was a ringing blow against slavery when it was a much softer blow against the transatlantic slave trade.

Spielberg's movie created a huge new interest in the *Amistad* story and brought welcome recognition to several groups that had been laboring in relative obscurity to resurrect the *Amistad* story in the public consciousness. Among them were the New Haven–based Connecticut Afro-American Historical Society, founded in 1971, and a new Amistad Committee, founded in 1988. Together they commissioned a monument to commemorate the one hundred and fiftieth anniversary of the *Amistad*. The fourteen-foot-high bronze relief sculpture of Cinque stands in front of New Haven City Hall, the site of the former jail that held Cinque and the others.

Foremost of the behind-the-scenes leaders is scholar and journalist Warren Q. Marr II, who has had a lifelong interest in the *Amistad*. While working for the modern incarnation of the American Missionary Association in the 1960s, Marr helped found the Amistad Research Center at Fisk University. The center is now located at Tulane University in New Orleans and holds more than ten million documents, the largest collection of human rights-related manuscript materials in the world.

The building of the Cinque statue led Marr and others on a fundraising drive to build a replica of the *Amistad* schooner. The $2.5 million schooner was launched at Mystic, Connecticut, on March 25, 2000. The dedication ceremony attracted people from many cultural, political, and religious backgrounds, including a contingent from Sierra Leone.

The schooner is berthed in New Haven and tours the world as an "educational ambassador." Amistad America, a nonprofit foundation that operates the ship, describes the replica as "a floating classroom, icon, and monument to the millions of souls that were broken or lost as a result of the transatlantic slave trade."

NOTES

Introduction
p. 9, par. 3, "Kale to John Quincy Adams" (January 4, 1841), Adams Family Papers, Massachusetts Historical Society.

p. 9, par. 5, Norton's diary entry for March 12, 1841, Group N. 367, Record Unit II, box 3, folder 18, John P. Norton Papers, Manuscripts and Archives, Sterling Memorial Library, Yale University. Cited in "The *Amistad* Test, Colonization and Abolition: The Role of New Haven and Yale" by Howard Jones, Yale Law School (2002).

Chapter 1
p. 11, par. 1, *New London Gazette* (August 26, 1839), University of Missouri School of Law Web site. http://www.law.umkc.edu/faculty/projects/ftrials/amistad/AMI_NEWS.HTM

p. 15, par. 5, "New Haven Population," State of Connecticut Office of Policy Management, Connecticut Population Projections, Series 95.1 (Revised November 13, 2001). http://www.cityofnewhaven.com/library/population.htm

p. 16, par. 4, Antony Dugdale, J. J. Fueser, and J. Celso de Castro Alves, "Yale, Slavery and Abolition," Amistad Committee, Inc. (2001). http://www.yaleslavery.org/Resources/timeline.html#t2

p. 16, par.4 , "Slavery in Connecticut," *New York Journal of Commerce* (January 5, 1841), Exploring *Amistad* at Mystic Seaport. http://amistad.mysticseaport.org/library/news

p. 17, par. 2, "The Story of Yale Abolitionists," Amistad

Committee, Inc. http://www.yaleslavery.org/Abolitionists/
abolit.html

p. 18, par. 2–p. 19, par. 2, "The Spanish Piratical Schooner
Amistad," *New London Gazette* (August 26, 1839), Exploring
Amistad at Mystic Seaport.
http://amistad.mysticseaport.org/library/news

p. 19, par. 5–p. 20, par. 2, *Thomas R. Gedney & c. v. The
Schooner Amistad, &c.*, Case files, U.S. District Court,
District of Connecticut, RG 21, National Archives and
Records Administration – Northeast Region (Boston).

p. 20, par. 4, "Implications of the *Amistad* Case, Cinquez,"
New York Morning Herald (September 17, 1839), Exploring
Amistad at Mystic Seaport.
http://amistad.mysticseaport.org/library/news

p. 20, par. 7, Jeremy Brecher, "The *Amistad* Incident," Amistad
America, Inc. http://www.amistadamerica.org

Sidebar

pp. 21–23, "They Made America," Public Broadcasting Service
(2004).

Bertram Wyatt-Brown, *Lewis Tappan and the Evangelical War
Against Slavery* (1969).

"The Mendi Mission," *The Oberlin Evangelist* (June 22, 1842).

Douglas O. Linder, "Stamped With Glory: Lewis Tappan and
the Africans of the *Amistad*," University of Missouri School
of Law Web site, 2000. http://www.law.umkc.edu/faculty/
projects/ftrials/trialheroes/Tappanessay.html

Marvis Olive Welch, *Prudence Crandall, A Biography*
(Manchester, Connecticut, 1983) and Samuel J. May, *Some
Recollections of the Anti Slavery Conflict* (Boston, 1869), cited
in Exploring *Amistad* at Mystic Seaport.
http://amistad.mysticseaport.org

p. 24, par. 2, "Lewis Tappan," Exploring *Amistad* at Mystic
Seaport. http://amistad.mysticseaport.org

p. 25, par. 2, "Funds Appeal, *New York Commercial Advertiser*
(September 5, 1839), Exploring *Amistad* at Mystic Seaport.
http://amistad.mysticseaport.org/library/news

p. 25, par. 3, "Implications of the *Amistad* Case, Cinquez," *New York Morning Herald* (September 17, 1839), Exploring *Amistad* at Mystic Seaport.
http://amistad.mysticseaport.org/library/news

p. 25, par. 4, L. N. Fowler, "Phrenological Developments of Joseph Cinquez, Alias Ginqua," *American Phrenological Journal and Miscellany*, vol. 2 (1840), pp. 136–138, Exploring *Amistad* at Mystic Seaport. http:// amistad.mysticseaport.org

p. 26, par. 2, "The Captured Africans," *New York Morning Herald* (September 18, 1839), Exploring *Amistad* at Mystic Seaport. http://amistad.mysticseaport.org/ library/news

p. 26, par.5, Pinckney's Treaty (1785).

p. 28, par. 2, Letter from Angel Calderon de la Barca to U.S. Secretary of State John Forsyth, September 6, 1839, Exploring *Amistad* at Mystic Seaport.
http://amistad.mysticseaport.org

p. 28, par. 3, "Martin Van Buren," AmericanPresident.org, University of Virginia's Miller Center of Public Affairs. http://ap.beta.polardesign.com/history/martinvanburen/ biography

p. 30, par. 3, "William Henry Harrison," AmericanPresident.org, University of Virginia's Miller Center of Public Affairs. http://www.americanpresident.org/history/william hharrison/biography/CampaignsElections.common.shtml

Chapter 2

p. 32, par. 1–p. 33, par. 5, "The Terrible Transformation," Public Broadcasting Service (PBS).
http://www.pbs.org/wgbh/aia/part1/1p263.html

p. 35, par. 2, Jay Coughtry, ed. adviser, "Papers of the American Slave Trade," Bethesda, MD: University Publications of America (1996).

p. 35, par. 3, "The Terrible Transformation."

p. 36, par. 1, 2, James Hall, M.D., "Abolition of the Slave Trade of Gallinas." Annual Report, The American Colonization Society, vol. 33 (1850), pp. 33–36, on the Exploring *Amistad* at Mystic Seaport Web site. http://amistad.mysticseaport. org/library/misc/am.col.gallinas.1.html

p. 36, par. 3, "The Terrible Transformation."

p. 37, par. 3, "The Last Slave Ships," Mel Fisher Maritime Heritage Society (2002). http://www.melfisher.org/lastslaveships/slaveships.htm

p. 37, par. 4, "The Terrible Transformation."

p. 38, par. 1, 2, Douglas Harper, "Slavery in the North," http://www.slavenorth.com/massachusetts.htm

p. 38, par. 3, "When Did Virginia Legalize Slavery?" Solutions, *Daily Press* (December 8, 2000). http://www.dailypress.com/extras/solutions/sol120800.htm

p. 38, par. 3, "The Terrible Transformation."

p. 39, par. 4, Stephen Krasner, "How Britain Ended Slavery Around the Globe, *Sovereignty: Organized Hypocrisy*" (Princeton, NJ: Princeton University Press, 1999).

p. 41, par. 2, Nigel Sadler, "Liberated Africans: Putting Right the Wrongs of the Past," Turks & Caicos National Museum. http://www.timespub.tc/Astrolabe/Archive/Winter%202003 04/liberated_africans.htm

p. 41, par. 4, Hugh Thomas, *The Slave Trade* (New York: Simon and Schuster, 1997), p. 583.

p. 42, par. 1, Nigel Sadler, "Liberated Africans: Putting Right the Wrongs of the Past."

p. 43, par. 3, "The War for States Rights." http://civilwar.bluegrass.net/secessioncrisis/200303.html

p. 44, par. 2, "Brotherly Love," Public Broadcasting Service (PBS). http://www.pbs.org/wgbh/aia/part3/3h511.html

p. 46, par. 1, "American Abolitionism," University of Indiana. http://americanabolitionist.liberalarts.iupui.edu

Chapter 3

p. 47, par. 1, "The Captured Africans of the *Amistad*," *New York Morning Herald* (October 4, 1839) p. 2, Exploring *Amistad* at Mystic Seaport. http://amistad.mysticseaport.org/library/news

p. 47, par. 3–4, "Incarcerated Captives," *New York Commercial Advertiser* (September 6, 1839), Exploring *Amistad* at Mystic Seaport. http://amistad.mysticseaport.org/library

p. 49, par. 1, "An Incident," *New York Commercial Advertiser*

(September 26, 1839), Exploring *Amistad* at Mystic Seaport. http://amistad.mysticseaport.org/library/news

p. 49, par. 4, "Letter from Lewis Tappan" (September 9, 1839), University of Missouri School of Law Web site. http://www.law.umkc.edu/faculty/projects/ftrials/amistad/ AMI_LTR.HTM

p. 50, par. 5, Douglas O. Linder, "Stamped With Glory: Lewis Tappan and the Africans of the *Amistad*," University of Missouri School of Law Web site, 2000. http://www.law.umkc.edu/faculty/projects/ftrials/trial heroes/Tappanessay.html

p. 51, par. 4, Douglas O. Linder, "Stamped With Glory: Lewis Tappan and the Africans of the *Amistad*."

p. 52, par. 2, Peter P. Hinks, "What is your story?: Howard Jones and Steven Spielberg on the History of the *Amistad* Conflict," on the Amistad America, Inc. Web site, 2004. http://www.Amistadamerica.org/index.cfm?fuseaction= home.viewPage&page_id=D93F3BD2-B7CD-7952-62C27 DADFC6F7166

p. 53, par. 1, 2, "Trial account," *Richmond Enquirer* (September 24, 1839), p. 2, Exploring *Amistad* at Mystic Seaport. http://amistad.mysticseaport.org/library/news

p. 53, par. 3, "The *Amistad* Circuit Court Trial," *New York Commercial Advertiser* (September 23, 1839), University of Missouri School of Law Web site. http://www.law.umkc.edu/faculty/projects/ftrials/amistad/ Ami_trialrep.html

Sidebar

pp. 54–57, "The Child Captives," Amistad America. http://www.Amistadamerica.org.
"Letter from Lewis Tappan (September 9, 1839), University of Missouri School of Law Web site. http://www.law. umkc.edu/faculty/projects/ftrials/amistad/AMI_LTR.HTM Abraham, Arthur. "The Amistad Revolt: An Historical Legacy of Sierra Leone and the United States," U.S. Department of State's Bureau of International Information Publication (1998).

Marlene D. Merrill, "Sarah Margru Kinson: The Two Worlds of an Amistad Captive," Oberlin Historical and Improvement Organization (2003).
"Mendis Depart," *New York Journal of Commerce*, November 27, 1841.

p. 58, par. 2, Trial record, University of Missouri School of Law Web site. http://www.law.umkc.edu/faculty/projects/ftrials/amistad/Ami_trialrep.html

p. 58, par. 3, "Case of the Captured Africans," *New York Morning Herald* (October 1, 1839), Exploring *Amistad* at Mystic Seaport. http://amistad.mysticseaport.org/library/news

p. 59, par. 3, "Case of the Captured Africans."

p. 59, par. 5, Douglas O. Linder, "Stamped With Glory: Lewis Tappan and the Africans of the *Amistad*."

p. 61, par. 1, "The Captured Africans," *New York Commercial Advertiser* (October 4, 1839), Exploring *Amistad* at Mystic Seaport. http://amistad.mysticseaport.org/library/news

p. 61, par. 4, Douglas O. Linder, "Stamped With Glory: Lewis Tappan and the Africans of the *Amistad*."

p. 62, par.5, "The several pleas of Sinqua, Burnah, et al.," (November 19, 1839) cited in "Incited by the Love of Liberty: The *Amistad* Captives and the Federal Courts," by Bruce A. Ragsdale, *Prologue*, vol. 35, no. 1 (Spring 2003).

p. 64, par. 3, *United States* v. *Amistad*, 40 U. S. 518 (1841).

p. 64, par. 4, Clifton Johnson, "The *Amistad* Case and its Consequences in US History," Amistad Research Center. http://www.amistadresearchcenter.org

p. 66, par. 1, 2, "Adams Letter on Amistad Africans," *New York Journal of Commerce* (December 25, 1839) p. 2, Exploring *Amistad* at Mystic Seaport. http://amistad.mysticseaport.org/library/news

Chapter 4
p. 67, par. 2, Douglas O. Linder, "Stamped With Glory: Lewis Tappan and the Africans of the *Amistad*," University of Missouri School of Law Web site, 2000.

http://www.law.umkc.edu/faculty/projects/ftrials/trial
heroes/Tappanessay.html

p. 68, par. 1, 2, "Extract of a letter from Rev. H. G. Ludlow, to
one of the Editors, dated New Haven, January 13, 1840,"
New York Journal of Commerce (January 15, 1840), Exploring
Amistad at Mystic Seaport. http://amistad.mysticseaport.
org/library/news

p. 69, par. 5–p. 70, par. 3, "African Testimony," *New York
Journal of Commerce* (January 10, 1840), p. 2, Exploring
Amistad at Mystic Seaport. http://amistad.mysticseaport.
org/library/news

p. 70, par. 4, Peter P. Hinks, "What is your story?: Howard
Jones and Steven Spielberg on the History of the *Amistad*
Conflict," Amistad America, Inc. (2004).
http://www.Amistadamerica.org/index.cfm?fuseaction=
home.viewPage&page_id=D93F3BD2-B7CD-7952-62C27
DADFC6F7166

p. 70, par. 5, "African Testimony," *New York Journal of
Commerce* (January 10, 1840), p. 2, Exploring *Amistad* at
Mystic Seaport. http://amistad.mysticseaport.
org/library/news

p. 70, par. 6, "Testimony of Antonio, January 9, 1840, U.S.
District Court, Connecticut," Exploring *Amistad* at Mystic
Seaport. http://amistad.mysticseaport.org/
library/court/district/1840.1.9.antoniotest.html

p. 71, par. 3–6, "A Decision at Last in the *Amistad* Case," *New
York Morning Herald* (January 15, 1840), Exploring *Amistad*
at Mystic Seaport. http://amistad.mysticseaport.org/
library/news

p. 72, par. 2, "Extract of a letter from Rev. H. G. Ludlow, to one
of the Editors, dated New Haven, January 13, 1840," *New
York Journal of Commerce* (January 15, 1840), Exploring
Amistad at Mystic Seaport. http://amistad.mysticseaport.
org/library/news

p. 72, par. 5, "Ruiz," *New York Morning Herald* (February 14,
1840) p. 2, Exploring *Amistad* at Mystic Seaport.
http://amistad.mysticseaport.org/library

p. 73, par. 3, "Motion to dismiss appeal," *United States* v. *Cinque*, April term, 1840, U.S. Circuit Court, District of Connecticut, RG 21, cited in Douglas O. Linder, "Stamped With Glory: Lewis Tappan and the Africans of the *Amistad*."

p. 73, par. 5, Douglas O. Linder, "Stamped With Glory: Lewis Tappan and the Africans of the *Amistad*."

Chapter 5
Sidebar

p. 77, par. 2, Richard Kluger, *Simple Justice* (New York: Alfred A. Knopf, 1976), p. 706.

p. 77, par. 3, John Marshall Harlan, dissent, *Plessy* v. *Ferguson*, 163 U.S. 537 (1896).

p. 78, par. 1, David Rudenstine, *The Day the Presses Stopped* (Berkeley: University of California Press, 1996), p. 301.

p. 78, par. 2, *New York Times* v. *United States*, 403 U.S. 713 (1971).

p. 78, par. 3, The National Security Archive, "The Pentagon Papers: Secrets, Lies and Audiotapes (The Nixon Tapes and the Supreme Court Tape)." http://www.gwu.edu/~nsarchiv/NSAEBB/NSAEBB48/supreme.html

p. 79, par. 1, Mark W. Janis, "Dred Scott and International Law," *Columbia Journal of Transnational Law* (May 20, 2005), p. 776, 43:763.

p. 80, par. 1, 2, *The Antelope*, 23 U. S. (10 Wheat.) at 118.

p. 81, par. 2, Douglas O. Linder, "Stamped With Glory: Lewis Tappan and the Africans of the *Amistad*," University of Missouri School of Law Web site, 2000. http://www.law.umkc.edu/faculty/projects/ftrials/trial heroes/Tappanessay.html

p. 81, par. 2, "History of the Court," Supreme Court Historical Society. http://www.supremecourthistory. org/02_history/subs_history/02_c05.html

p. 81, par. 3, "Joseph Story," Exploring *Amistad* at Mystic Seaport. http://amistad.mysticseaport.org

p. 85, par. 1, "Timeline," Exploring *Amistad* at Mystic Seaport. http://amistad.mysticseaport.org/timeline/courttimeline.html

Sidebar

pp. 86–88, The Supreme Court Historical Society
http://www.supremecourthistory.org
Administrative Office of the U.S. Courts
http://www.uscourts.gov
Iowa Court Information System
http://www.judicial.state.ia.us/students/6
There is also a diagram on the last Web site.

p. 89, par. 4–p. 91, par. 3, Henry D. Gilpin arguments, *United States* v. *Amistad*, 40 U. S. 518 (1841).

Chapter 6

p. 92, par. 2–97, par. 3, Roger S. Baldwin arguments, *United States* v. *Amistad*, 40 U. S. 518 (1841).

p. 98, par. 2–98, par. 5; p. 99, par. 3, 4; p. 102, par. 1–103, par. 1, John Quincy Adams arguments, *United States* v. *Amistad*, 40 U. S. 518 (1841).

Sidebar

pp. 100–101, "Justice Joseph Story," in Famous American Trials: Amistad Trials by Douglas O. Linder. University of Missouri School of Law Web site, 1998. http://www.law.umkc.edu/faculty/projects/ftrials/amistad/AMI_BSTO.HTM
Pennsylvania Avenue National Historic Park Web site.
http://www.nps.gov/paav/hotels.htm
Sarah Luria, "National Domesticity in the Early Republic: Washington, D.C." Common-Place, 3: 4 (July 2003).
http://www.common-place.org/vol-03/no-04/washington
The History of the Dacor Bacon House." http://www.dacorbacon.org/DBHF/Dacor_Bacon_House.htm

p. 103, par. 3, "Adams' Argument," *New York Journal of Commerce*, February 25, 1841, on Exploring *Amistad* at Mystic Seaport Web site. http://amistad.mysticseaport.org/library/news/nyjc/1841.02.25.adams.argu.html

Chapter 7

p. 105–107, par. 4, *United States* v. *Amistad*, 40 U. S. 518 (1841).

p. 107, par. 5, Douglas O. Linder, "Stamped With Glory: Lewis Tappan and the Africans of the *Amistad*," University of Missouri School of Law Web site, 2000. http://www.law.umkc.edu/faculty/projects/ftrials/trial heroes/Tappanessay.html

p. 108, par. 2, 3, "Timeline: Legal Path of the *Amistad* Case: 1839–1845," Exploring *Amistad* at Mystic Seaport. http://amistad.mysticseaport.org

p. 109, par. 3, *Dred Scott* v. *Sandford*, 60 U. S. 393 (1857).

p. 111, par. 2, Emancipation Proclamation.

p. 111, par. 3, Amendment 14, U.S. Constitution.

p. 112, par. 1, Joshua Giddings, "Speech to the House on the *Amistad* Question" (December 21, 1853), cited in *The Amistad Africans and America: A Study in Response*, by Peter J. Iverson, University of Wisconsin (1969), Exploring *Amistad* at Mystic Seaport. http://amistad.mysticseaport.org

p. 112, par. 2, "Mendis Perform," *New York Herald* (May 15, 1841), and "Meetings of the Liberated Africans," *Colored American* (May 22, 1841), Exploring *Amistad* at Mystic Seaport. http://amistad.mysticseaport.org/library/news

p. 114, par. 1, Douglas O. Linder, "Stamped With Glory: Lewis Tappan and the Africans of the *Amistad*."

p. 114, par. 3, Clifton Johnson, "The *Amistad* Case and its Consequences in US History," Amistad Research Center. http://www.amistadresearchcenter.org

p. 114, par. 4, "United Church of Christ and *Amistad*," *Worldwide Faith News* (March 29, 2000). http://www.wfn.org/2000/03/msg00267.html

p. 115, par. 2, "Early African American Missionaries: Treasures of the Day Missions Library," Yale University Divinity School Library. http://www.library.yale.edu/div/AfricanAmericanMissionaries.ppt

p. 115, par. 3, Douglas O. Linder, "Stamped With Glory: Lewis Tappan and the Africans of the *Amistad*."

p. 115, par. 4, Jeremy Brecher, "The *Amistad* Incident," Amistad America, Inc. http://www.amistadamerica.org

p. 117, par. 4, "*Amistad* Voyage to Freedom," Exploring *Amistad* at Mystic Seaport. http://amistad.mysticseaport.org

p. 117, par. 4, Mission statement, Amistad America, Inc. http://www.amistadamerica.org

All Web sites accessible as of January 23, 2006.

furTHer informaTion

AUDIO/VIDEO
Amistad *CD-Rom*, Amistad America, Inc., no date.
The Amistad *Revolt*, video, Amistad Committee, 1995.
I Remember the Amistad, video, United Church of Christ, no date.
Spielberg, Steven, director. Amistad, film, Dreamworks, 1997.
The Voyage of La Amistad: *A Quest for Freedom*, video, MPI Teleproductions, 2005.

BOOKS
Angelou, Maya, Debbie Allen, and Steven Spielberg, eds. Amistad: *Give Us Free*. New York: Newmarket Press, 1998.
Cable, Mary. *Black Odyssey: The Case of the Slave Ship* Amistad. New York: Penguin Books, 1998.
Jones, Howard. *Mutiny on the* Amistad: *The Saga of a Slave Revolt and Its Impact on American Abolition, Law, and Diplomacy*. New York: Oxford University Press, 1997.
Jurmain, Suzanne. *Freedom's Sons: The True Story of the* Amistad *Mutiny*. New York: Lothrop, Lee and Shepard Books, 1998.
McKissack, Patricia C. Amistad: *The Story of a Slave Ship*. New York: Grosset & Dunlap, 2005.
Myers, Walter Dean. Amistad: *A Long Road to Freedom*. New York: Dutton Books, 1998.

Osagie, Iyunolu Folayan. *The* Amistad *Revolt: Memory, Slavery, and the Politics of Identity in the United States and Sierra Leone*. Athens: University of Georgia Press, 2000.

Owens, William A. *Black Mutiny: The Revolt on the Schooner* Amistad. Baltimore: Black Classic Press, 1997.

Sterne, Emma Gelders. *Story of the* Amistad. Hempstead, TX: Sagebrush, 2001.

Zeinert, Karen. *The* Amistad *Slave Revolt and American Abolition*. Hempstead, TX: Sagebrush, 1997.

WEB SITES

African American Odyssey, Library of Congress.
http://lcweb2.loc.gov/ammem/aaohtml/aohome.html

Amistad America, Inc.
http://www.amistadamerica.org

The *Amistad*—Part 2: Hollywood! (Utopia Lesson Plans).
http://utopia.utexas.edu/lesson_plans/2005/puckett_amistad_2.php

Amistad Research Center at Tulane University.
http://amistadresearchcenter.org/ama-research.htm

The *Amistad* Trial, University of Missouri School of Law Web site. http://www.law.umkc.edu/faculty/projects/ftrials/amistad/AMISTD.HTM

Connecticut: *Amistad* Trail (Mystic Media, Inc.).
http://visitconnecticut.com/amistad.htm

Exploring *Amistad* (Mystic Seaport).
http://amistad.mysticseaport.org

FindLaw (U.S. Supreme Court Cases).
http://www.findlaw.com/casecode/supreme.html

Harper, Douglas: Slavery in the North.
http://www.slavenorth.com/index.html

Legal Information Institute, Cornell Law School.
http://www.law.cornell.edu

National Park Service: *Amistad*: Seeking Freedom in
Connecticut.
http://www.cr.nps.gov/nr/travel/amistad/index.htm

Oyez Project: U.S. Supreme Court Multimedia Web Site.
http://www.oyez.org/oyez/frontpage

Supreme Court of the United States.
http://www.supremecourtus.gov

Supreme Court Historical Society.
http://www.supremecourthistory.org

U.S. Department of State's Bureau of International
Information Programs.
http://usinfo.state.gov/products/pubs/amistad/

U.S. National Archives and Records Administration.
http://www.archives.gov/education/lessons/amistad

BIBLIOGRaPHY

ARTICLES

Abraham, Arthur. "The *Amistad* Revolt: An Historical Legacy of Sierra Leone and the United States." U.S. Department of State's Bureau of International Information Publication (1998).

"Adams Letter on *Amistad* Africans." *New York Journal of Commerce* (December 25, 1839), p. 2.

"African Testimony." *New York Journal of Commerce* (January 10, 1840).

"The *Amistad* Case and the Federal Courts." *The Court Historian*. Federal Judicial History Office, no. 9 (March 1998).

"The *Amistad* Circuit Court Trial." *New York Commercial Advertiser* (September 23, 1839).

Brecher, Jeremy. "The *Amistad* Incident." Amistad America, Inc. http://www. amistadamerica.org

"The Captured Africans of the *Amistad*." *New York Morning Herald* (October 4, 1839), p. 2.

"Case of the Captured Africans." *New York Morning Herald* (October 1, 1839).

"A Decision at Last in the *Amistad* Case." *New York Morning Herald* (January 15, 1840).

Dugdale, Antony; J. J. Fueser, and J. Celso de Castro Alves. "Yale, Slavery and Abolition." Amistad Committee, Inc. (2001).

"Extract of a letter from Rev. H. G. Ludlow, to one of the

Editors, dated New Haven, Jan. 13, 1840." *New York Journal of Commerce* (January 15, 1840).

Hall, James, M.D. "Abolition of the Slave Trade of Gallinas." Annual Report, *The American Colonization Society*, vol. 33 (1850).

Harper, Douglas. "Slavery in the North." http://www. slavenorth.com/massachusetts.htm

Hinks, Peter P. "What is your story?: Howard Jones and Steven Spielberg on the History of the *Amistad* Conflict." Amistad America, Inc., 2004. http://www. Amistadamerica.org/index.cfm?fuseaction=home.vie wPage&page_id=D93F3BD2-B7CD-7952-62C27DAD FC6F7166

Hopkins, Desiree R. "Abolition of the Atlantic Slave Trade in the United States." Trade Environment Database (TED) Projects (1999).

"Implications of the *Amistad* Case, Cinquez." *New York Morning Herald* (September 17, 1839).

"Incarcerated Captives." *New York Commercial Advertiser* (September 6, 1839).

"An Incident." *New York Commercial Advertiser* (September 26, 1839).

Janis, Mark W. "Dred Scott and International Law." *Columbia Journal of Transnational Law* (May 20, 2005) p. 776, 43:763.

Johnson, Clifton. "The *Amistad* Case and its Consequences in US History." Amistad Research Center. http://www.amistadresearchcenter.org

Jones, Howard. "The *Amistad* Test, Colonization and Abolition: The Role of New Haven and Yale." Yale Law School (2002).

Lane, Calvin. "The African Squadron, the U.S. Navy and the Slave Trade, 1820–1862." Exploring *Amistad* at Mystic Seaport. http://amistad.mysticseaport.org/ library/news

"The Last Slave Ships." Mel Fisher Maritime Heritage Society (2002).

"Letter from Lewis Tappan" (September 9, 1839). University of Missouri School of Law Web site. http://www.law.umkc.edu/faculty/projects/ftrials/amistad/AMI_LTR.HTM

Linder, Douglas O. "Stamped With Glory: Lewis Tappan and the Africans of the *Amistad*." University of Missouri School of Law Web site, 2000. http://www.law.umkc.edu/faculty/projects/ftrials/trial heroes/Tappanessay.html

"Meetings of the Liberated Africans." *Colored American* (May 22, 1841).

"Mendis Perform." *New York Herald* (May 15, 1841).

New London Gazette (August 26, 1839).

Ragsdale, Bruce A. "Incited by the Love of Liberty: The *Amistad* Captives and the Federal Courts." *Prologue*, vol. 35, no. 1 (Spring 2003).

"Ruiz." *New York Morning Herald* (February 14, 1840), p. 2.

Sadler, Nigel. "Liberated Africans: Putting Right the Wrongs of the Past." Turks & Caicos National Museum.

"Slavery in Connecticut." *New York Journal of Commerce* (January 5, 1841).

"The Terrible Transformation." Public Broadcasting Service (PBS) (1998, 1999).

"Trial account." *Richmond Enquirer* (September 24, 1839), p. 2.

"United Church of Christ and *Amistad*." *Worldwide Faith News* (March 29, 2000).

BOOKS/BOOKLETS

Adams, Charles Francis, ed. *Memoirs of John Quincy Adams, Comprising Portions of His Diary from 1795 to 1848*, 12 vols. (Philadelphia: Lippincott, 1874–77).

Coughtry, Jay, ed. adviser. "Papers of the American Slave

Trade." (Bethesda, MD: University Publications of America, 1996).

Iverson, Peter J. *The* Amistad *Africans and America: A Study in Response.* (Madison: University of Wisconsin, 1969).

Jones, Howard. *Mutiny on the* Amistad: *The Saga of a Slave Revolt and Its Impact on American Abolition, Law, and Diplomacy.* (New York: Oxford University Press, 1997).

Krasner, Stephen. "How Britain Ended Slavery Around the Globe, *Sovereignty: Organized Hypocrisy.*" (Princeton, NJ: Princeton University Press, 1999).

Supreme Court Historical Society. "Supreme Court of the United States" (booklet).

Thomas, Hugh. *The Slave Trade* (New York: Simon and Schuster, 1997).

Vogel, Robert. *Without Consent or Contract.* (New York: W.W. Norton, 1989).

COURT CASES/DOCUMENTS

The African Captives: Trial of the Prisoners of the "Amistad" on the Writ of Habeas Corpus before the Circuit Court of the United States for the District of Connecticut, at Hartford; Judges Thompson and Judson, September Term, 1839. (New York: American Anti-slavery Society, 1839).

The African Repository and Colonial Journal. (Washington, D.C.: American Colonization Society, monthly).

The Antelope, 23 U. S. 66 (1825).

Dred Scott v. *Sandford,* 60 U. S. 393 (1857).

Emancipation Proclamation.

H. Exec. Doc. 185. U.S. Congress, House Executive Documents, no. 185, 26th Cong., 1st sess. (1840).

"Motion to dismiss appeal." *United States* v. *Cinque*, April term, 1840, U.S. Circuit Court, District of Connecticut.

"New Haven Population." State of Connecticut Office of Policy Management. Connecticut Population Projections, Series 95.1 (Revised November 13, 2001).

Pinckney's Treaty (1785).

Testimony of Antonio, January 9, 1840, U.S. District Court, Connecticut.

Trial record, University of Missouri School of Law, http://www.law.umkc.edu/faculty/projects/ftrials/amistad/Ami_trialrep.html

United States vs. *The Amistad*, 40 U. S. 518 (1841).

AUDIO/VIDEO
Amistad (Dreamworks, 1997)(Steven Spielberg, Director).

WEB SITES
"Abolition of the Atlantic Slave Trade in the United States," Trade Environment Database (TED) Projects (Desiree R. Hopkins).
http://www.american.edu/projects/mandala/TED/slave.htm

African American Odyssey, Library of Congress.
http://lcweb2.loc.gov/ammem/aaohtml/aohome.html

AmericanPresident.org, University of Virginia's Miller Center of Public Affairs.
http://www.americanpresident.org

Amistad I and *Amistad* II: 160 years and two court cases.
http://www.law.cornell.edu/background/amistad/
amistad3.html

Amistad America, Inc. http://www.amistadamerica.org

The *Amistad*—Part 2: Hollywood! (Utopia Lesson Plans).
http://utopia.utexas.edu/lesson_plans/2005/puckett_
amistad_2.php

Amistad Research Center at Tulane University.
http://amistadresearchcenter.org/ama-research.htm

The *Amistad* Trial, University of Missouri School of Law.
http://www.law.umkc.edu/faculty/projects/ftrials/amistad/
AMISTD.HTM

Connecticut: *Amistad* Trail (Mystic Media, Inc.).
http://visitconnecticut.com/amistad.htm

Exploring *Amistad* (Mystic Seaport).
http://amistad.mysticseaport.org

FindLaw (U.S. Supreme Court Cases).
http://www.findlaw.com/casecode/supreme.html

Landmark Cases of the U.S. Supreme Court.
http://www.landmarkcases.org

"The Last Slave Ships," Mel Fisher Maritime Heritage
Society (2002).
http://www.melfisher.org/lastslaveships/slaveships.htm

Legal Information Institute, Cornell Law School.
http://www.law.cornell.edu

National Park Service: *Amistad*: Seeking Freedom in
Connecticut.
http://www.cr.nps.gov/nr/travel/amistad/index.htm

Oyez Project: U.S. Supreme Court Multimedia Web Site.
http://www.oyez.org/oyez/frontpage

Supreme Court of the United States.
http://www.supremecourtus.gov

Supreme Court Historical Society.
http://www.supremecourthistory.org

"The Terrible Transformation," Public Broadcasting
Service (PBS). http://www.pbs.org/wgbh/aia/part1/
1p263.html

U.S. Department of State's Bureau of International
Information Programs.
http://usinfo.state.gov/products/pubs/amistad

U.S. National Archives and Records Administration
http://www.archives.gov/education/lessons/amistad

All Web sites accessible as of January 23, 2006.

index

Page numbers in **boldface** are illustrations, tables, and charts.

aBOUT THE auTHor

SUSAN DUDLEY GOLD has written more than three dozen books for middle-school and high-school students on a variety of topics, including American history, health issues, law, and space. Her most recent works for Benchmark Books are *Gun Control* in the Open for Debate series, and *Roe v. Wade: A Woman's Choice?*, *Brown v. Board of Education: Separate but Equal?*, *The Pentagon Papers: National Security or the Right to Know*, *Engel v. Vitale: Prayer in the Schools*, *Korematsu v. United States: Japanese-American Internment*, and *Vernonia School District v. Acton: Drug Testing in the Schools*—all in the Supreme Court Milestones series. She is currently working on two more books about Supreme Court cases.

Susan Gold has also written several books on Maine history. Among her many careers in journalism are stints as a reporter for a daily newspaper, managing editor of two statewide business magazines, and freelance writer for several regional publications. She and her husband, John Gold, own and operate a Web design and publishing business. Susan has received numerous awards for her writing and design work. In 2001 she received a Jefferson Award for community service in recognition of her work with a support group for people with chronic pain, which she founded in 1993. Susan and her husband, also a children's book author, live in Maine. They have one son, Samuel.